In the Footsteps of
Florence Nightingale

In the Footsteps of Florence Nightingale

Memoirs of a QA

Margaret Thomas

Dollarbird

 Dollarbird

First published in 2020
by Dollarbird, an imprint of Monsoon Books Ltd
www.dollarbird.co.uk
www.monsoonbooks.co.uk

No.1 The Lodge, Burrough Court,
Burrough on the Hill, Melton Mowbray LE14 2QS, UK.

ISBN (paperback): 978-1-912049-64-6
ISBN (ebook): 978-1-912049-65-3

Copyright©Margaret Thomas, 2020

The moral right of the author has been asserted.

All rights reserved. No part of this publication may be reproduced, stored in a retrieval system, or transmitted, in any form or by any means without the prior written permission of the publisher, nor be otherwise circulated in any form of binding or cover other than that in which it is published and without a similar condition being imposed on the subsequent purchaser.

Cover design by Cover Kitchen.

Photographs courtesy of Margaret Thomas.

A Cataloguing-in-Publication data record is available from the British Library.

Printed and bound in Great Britain by Clays Ltd, Elcograf S.p.A.
22 21 20   1 2 3

To my son, Ian,
who knew little of what his mum did
before he was born.

Acknowledgements

My sincere thanks to Elizabeth Bradshaw, Jean Loebl, Pauline Hay and Stephen Smith, without whose help and encouragement these memories would not have been completed.

During my research I referred to a number of publications on the history of QARANC and would like to highlight two books in particular: *History of the QARANC* by Juliet Piggott and *The Will to Live* by Sir John Smythe.

Contents

Summoned before the W.I.

1983

It all began one afternoon on the way home from Chesterfield Royal Hospital. Jenny Heathcote was sitting next to me on the bus; we both worked part-time. I had been 'scrubbed' at the theatre table from 8.30 that morning and was exceedingly weary.

'Margaret, would you come and talk to our W.I. about your time in the army?'

'Oh, Jenny, I couldn't possibly. I wouldn't know what to say.'

'Well, would you go away and think about it?'

It would have been churlish to say no to the Women's Institute again. 'Possibly, but I would need time.'

'Take as long as you like.'

I had resigned my commission in the Queen Alexandra's Royal Army Nursing Corps (QARANC) in January 1972 on family grounds to await the birth of our son in April. In

August our healthy son was four months old and on the 4th my husband suffered his first major heart attack and wasn't expected to survive. I mentally pulled down the blinds on the previous sixteen years of my life. That part was over and at thirty-nine years of age I had a new baby and a very sick husband – many new challenges lay ahead.

One quiet afternoon I sat at the kitchen table with a blank sheet of paper and put down the seven postings I'd had in various parts of the world – that was all I could remember. With my head in my hands I was thinking where did one start to interest thirty ladies at 2.30 on a Thursday afternoon: with a brief history of the QARANC, nicknamed the QAs? A look at how it all began in 1854 when Florence Nightingale was asked to start an army nursing service at Selimiye Barracks, the makeshift hospital for the soldiers of the Crimean War, in Scutari (modern-day Istanbul)? Perhaps a look at the scarlet and grey uniform with the starched white veil and the history of the scarlet tippet so special to the forces of the crown, the only visual aid available?

Blank pieces of paper were left around the house and with some concentration, slowly but surely over the next few months, while peeling potatoes at the sink, sewing quietly in the work room and just before falling asleep at night, the memories started to emerge and were noted down: the square bashing; the preparation of operating theatre supplies for Suez 1956; something nasty in the bathroom in Ghana; working with the Canadians in a shared military hospital in Germany; working all day and all night in theatres in Singapore with casualties being flown in from Borneo; ceremonial duties in London at 'The Trooping' and the Festival of Remembrance.

It was all there along with the happy, sad and sometimes hilarious incidents with service patients if only I could recall, compile and deliver it in a competent manner. A date was fixed for the talk and although it was impossible to know how it would go, it would all be over by 4 pm and I could sleep well in my bed that night.

As the meeting was just up the road I wore the QA indoor uniform but carried the veil. I spoke for too long – nearly an hour – but you could have heard a pin drop. I didn't realise one received a vote of thanks – that was nice, the hot cup of tea and cake nicer still.

On the way home I called in to my neighbour Sarah, a retired theatre sister, and over a cup of tea I told her I wasn't sure how it had gone but that I was glad it was all over and that I was off home to change and put my feet up.

As I walked in through the door the phone was ringing: could I come and give the same talk to another W.I. group? The phone kept ringing, what had I started?!

1

Childhood Ambitions

Born at Crookes in Sheffield in 1933, my childhood was spent in Nether Edge and I went to Abbeydale Grammar School. In the fourth year we were shown a nurse recruiting film called 'Student Nurse', filmed at the new and modern Birmingham Queen Elizabeth Hospital, which had opened in 1937. I was enthralled with it all and vowed that that was where I wanted to train. (I still have a rare copy of that recruitment video.)

I had wanted to nurse since, as a small child, I watched my father pierce my mother's ears in the kitchen with an aseptic technique I found fascinating – I had even run and fetched a small stool to stand on so that I could watch more closely! Mum wasn't pleased!

In the big snow of 1947 we used to do our homework and then go sledging on the very steep hills on Nether Edge. A young man helping me pull my sledge up the glacier of Oak Hill asked me what I was going to do when I left school.

'Oh! I'm going to be a nurse,' I replied. Arriving home for supper I announced to Mum and Dad that I was going to be a nurse and there was an ominous silence – they were horrified. Both born in Victorian times they had their reasons. Mum thought it was 'not quite nice' and that a domestic science teacher would be a much more respectable job. Father was a dear, kind man who had survived the horrors of three years in the trenches of the First World War. Having been injured either by the horses (he was Royal Field Artillery) or shot at by the Germans, he had been in and out of field hospitals at regular intervals. His family were cabinetmakers, so he was often asked if he could make an adaptor for the operating theatre table or put up another shelf before returning to his unit, as a consequence of which, I think, he saw too much in wards and operating theatres of the conditions under which QAs and VADs (Voluntary Aid Detachment civilians providing nursing care) worked. I believe he saw a lot of DOTs (death on the table) as he would never agree to having an anaesthetic for the rest of his life and was terrified when Mum had to go in for an operation. I think he had visions of his little girl in the same conditions.

I realised I had made a faux pas and changed the subject. On my return to school I quietly dropped Domestic Science (Mum found out years later) and asked to take three extra sciences available, which was to be a tremendous help later on. Passing School Certificate at sixteen, I applied to the

Queen Elizabeth Hospital (QEH) to start at eighteen years of age. My father drove me to Birmingham for the interview and I was accepted for April 1951. Meanwhile, I worked at a school day nursery for three- to five-year-olds.

I was at QEH for four years, the final year turning out to be the important one. As a student nurse I was sick when I should have gone for experience in the general theatre for six weeks. When well again I found to my disgust that I was to be sent to Ear Nose and Throat theatres. 'Dirty old ENT' we used to call it, but when I started I found I was fascinated by the technical side of theatre work. We had advanced surgery from America, performing 'fenestrations' using a superb Zeiss microscope in an attempt to cure deafness, routine tonsils and adenoids, nose jobs, and laryngectomies for cancers. Later, in 1954, we performed many mastoidectomies for chronic ear infections, which we traced back to post war, when a high enough dose of the new drug penicillin was not given – symptoms disappeared but the infection stayed quietly eating away at the bone. I did thirty cases in one month alone when Sister was off sick.

I took to it all like a duck to water and loved every frightening minute of it as a student. The staff nurse went off sick and I then had to work alongside Sister and at the end of eight weeks she asked me if I would like to come back as her staff nurse when I passed my finals.

'Oh, yes, please!'

ENT, rather like gynae, had never caught up with the backlog left over from the war so they had decided to start a postgraduate course and I was asked if I would like to enrol. Why not? The aim was to train departmental sisters capable of doing routine doctors' work in outpatients, examining ears, diagnosing common ailments and treating. We would also be capable of running the ward or the operating theatre if required. Anatomy and physiology of head and neck was done with a doctor doing his fellowship – useful as we tested each other in theatre when operating. We had written and oral examinations with outside consultants from Worcester. The petrous portion of the temporal bone, which protects the inner ear, was thrown to us and we had to describe every nook and cranny carrying nerves and blood vessels, etc. On passing the course we became members of the Midland Association of Otology with a certificate and lovely badge; little did I realise what an important part this certificate would play in my future professional life.

Training over, what was I to do now? My pay in '55 was £13 a month and the first priority was to obtain a decent wage and secondly to travel. The naval nurses had a very attractive tricorn hat with a white top which I rather fancied, so I applied. I received a curt reply; I had to be twenty-five years old and have midwifery. Princess Mary's (Princess

Mary's Royal Air Force Nursing Service, the nursing branch of the British Royal Air Force) also had a nice tricorn without the white top, but again no go, one had to be twenty-three years old and have midwifery. In desperation I wrote to the QAs. Yes! They would let me apply at twenty-two years old with a postgraduate certificate of any sort. Terrible hat!

I found I slipped into army nursing like slipping on an old glove. Only in recent years have I found out why. The matron asked to commission the new Queen Elizabeth Hospital Birmingham in 1937 had been a VAD in WWI and had been awarded the Associate Membership of the Royal Red Cross and had then gone on to do full nurse training at the Nightingale School of Nursing at St. Thomas's Hospital in London. She then slowly climbed the ladder in several appointments before being asked to come and start the Queen Elizabeth Hospital. The QEH had military wards during the war and had taken casualties from Dunkirk and then D-Day.

In 1940 the matron had wished to get married, but in those days it was not allowed for a matron to be a married woman and so she handed over to a new matron, who in the future would become Dame Catherine Smalldon. But her legacy lived on, the QEH was run as a military hospital even to nurses counting the knives, forks and spoons all set out on the kitchen hotplate before going off duty on late shift at 11 pm. On three occasions in the QAs, in three different hospitals, three different matrons sent for me and asked me to go to a certain ward and 'sort it out and bring it up to standard'. Why me, I used to ask myself, but now I know. Preparing for Matron's round and Commanding Officer's inspection was second nature to me – I'd had four years training before I joined the QAs.

2

In the Footsteps
of Florence Nightingale

To understand a little of what it is like in the QAs one must appreciate the great tradition behind the Corps and how it all began. Very quickly we must go back to 1854 when Florence Nightingale was asked by Sydney Herbert, the Secretary for War, to take a party of nurses to the Crimea to organise and supervise nursing in the barracks at Scutari being used as a military hospital.

This had come about because William Howard Russell of *The Times* had reported the horrendous conditions for the soldiers at Scutari. There were no dressers, nurses, no bandages, and sick and wounded were lying on filth-covered floors. There was little food, water and medical supplies. Four miles of wounded and dying soldiers. Hygiene was non-existent and I read one could smell the hospital ten miles away when the wind was in the wrong direction.

Florence Nightingale, born into a family of gentle birth, much to her family's distress broke away from the conventional mores of the time and twice went to the

Keiserworth Institute of Deaconesses in Germany to study nursing at first hand and adding practical experience to her knowledge of hygiene and sanitation. She had also done the grand tour and in European cities asked permission to visit nursing orders and for their advice on the running of those establishments.

She was a highly intelligent and religious young woman and more than anyone in history improved the lot of the British soldier and in civilian life her teachings and influences are still acknowledged to this day.

Finding the right type of nurse to go with her to the Crimea was a problem. Any person could call herself a nurse – a prostitute or alcoholic – think of Sarah Gamp in Dickens. Naturally many came from the nursing orders in London. They also had to agree to obey her commands, as she had to work within the system if it was to be a success.

She and thirty-eight nurses arrived in Scutari in October 1854. Having her own money she was able to buy certain stores and provisions before leaving and on arrival to purchase vegetables and arrowroot to make invalid food for the patients when permission was given. They made dressings and bandages and gradually began to bring some order out of the chaos, and eventually were allowed to give tender loving care to the patients. The filthy, foul uniforms were taken off, they were washed, wounds were dressed and the dying were comforted. The new army nursing service had begun.

On her return a fund was started by the grateful public, which resulted in the first nurse training school in the UK: The Nightingale School of Nursing at St. Thomas's Hospital in London. She was asked to work for the Royal Commission on the Health of the Army and also the Royal Sanitary Commission, where her experiences would re-organise the drains of the military hospitals. Her meticulous statistics kept throughout the war produced the first pie-chart showing that 70% of soldiers died of infection and not of wounds of battle, which greatly saddened her.

She became the architect of military hospitals that were easy to work in: large light airy wards always built to let in any breeze available passing across the wards and keeping them cool in the heat of the tropics. Large windows in Sister's office gave an excellent view of all the things going on in the wards – no recovery wards and high-tech intensive care in those days, or most of mine for that matter. Careful observations were critical which was a large part of our training. Her 'Cleanliness is next to Godliness' is just as relevant today.

After Queen Victoria's death King Edward VII ascended the throne and in 1902 Queen Alexandra accepted the invitation to become the first president of the new Queen

Alexandra's Imperial Military Nursing Service. She designed the QA medal in silver, hung on a scarlet and grey ribbon, to be worn on the right-hand side of the scarlet tippet on grey dress. It was made up of a Maltese Cross with an Imperial Crown on the top, taken from the House of Denmark, with the name of the service inscribed round the edge. Our motto was to be *Sub Cruce Candida* – 'under the white cross', taken from the flag of Denmark.

After WWII it was decided that the women's services would become an integral part of the British Army and in 1949 we became the Queen Alexandra's Royal Army Nursing Corps (QARANC, or QAs for short). We were now subject to military law; we could be court-martialled if we misbehaved. Entry could be as young as twenty-two years providing one had a recognised postgraduate certificate. If one's work was satisfactory one could be approached to become a regular officer after five to six years, and on passing junior and senior officer's promotion exams and having satisfactory annual confidential reports, the dizzy heights of becoming the matron-in-chief in the rank of brigadier could lie ahead. A minimum pension at sixteen years was now available to us – a marvellous career prospect in 1949. In 1950 we started training our own nurses for SEN (State Enrolled Nursing) and SRN (State Registered Nursing).

All through the history of the Corps there seems to

have been a special relationship between the troops and the sisters – a mutual respect and at times one seems to become a combination of 'mum' and that old-fashioned word 'sweetheart', depending on the age of the soldier and the severity of the sickness at the time. Sexual harassment was unknown and no bad language was ever heard in the wards. This was a marvellous working environment with total courtesy from all ranks – perhaps not fully appreciated until one had left the Corps. The only exception was to be two Canadian soldiers who overstepped the mark and I dealt with them in my own way.

3

Surrey

1955

On 10th August 1955 I arrived at the QARANC Training Centre at Hindhead in Surrey, an old hutted Canadian Camp left over from the War; very hot in summer, freezing cold in winter with old-fashioned heating stoves in the accommodation blocks that had to be stoked regularly by batwomen to keep going.

We had three weeks' training ahead of us to lick us all into shape to go to our hospitals. Square bashing was not a problem as I'd done a great deal in the Girl Guides, monthly Church parades and annual Empire Day parades through Sheffield town centre. We lived in khaki battle-dress top and skirt, khaki lisle stockings, new caps on our heads and blister-making beetle crushers on our feet. It was a very hot August but we were only allowed 'shirt sleeve order' on certain days and never on visits outside to other camps.

Weekends we shivered in our beds with temperatures

of 103°F to 104°F after very unpleasant inoculations and vaccinations. Lessons in QA administration, military law and all its rules and regulations regarding other ranks in hospitals followed. We found that processing and documentation of patients once learned, one could run a ward anywhere in the world as all army forms and books were universal. How sensible.

On the final Friday of the course we were to have lunch, finish our packing and report in civvies to the lecture room at 2 pm for our senior tutor to give us our final results and send us on our way. The door opened promptly on the dot of 2 pm and as we rose to our feet. Dear kind Col. Bennett sailed in like the proverbial ship in full sail and we all gasped! Dressed in scarlet and grey and wearing the standard white veil, rows of medal ribbons on the left side of her tippet and the QA medal on the right, the impact was quite astonishing and in later years I was to realise the effect we had on the troops coming in from a filthy battlefield and finding immaculately turned-out nurses to administer tender loving care to them. We had all passed our exams and she wished us well in our new postings and said finally she had a message from Florence Nightingale for us, which had been given to army nurses on the eve of the Egyptian Campaign in 1882. This was a surprise.

'Remember when you are far away up country, possibly the only English woman there, that these men will note and remember your every action not only as a nurse but as a woman.

Your life to them will be as rings a pebble makes when thrown into a pool reaching far and wide, each ripple gone beyond our grasp yet remembered almost to exaggeration by those soldiers lying helpless in their sickness.

See that your every word and act is worthy of your profession and your womanhood. God guard you in His safe keeping and make you worthy of His trust in our Soldiers.'

What a great tradition of the QAs, and an awesome responsibility had been given to us before we were sent on our way to our first military hospital. All of it as relevant today as it was over a hundred years ago.

4

Colchester

August 1955 – April 1957

On arrival at Colchester Military Hospital the taxi dropped me at Peabody Building as instructed. A beautiful new sisters' mess was being built so the sisters (including the matron) were scattered in various buildings.

The first person I set eyes on was a QA on a bicycle hurtling downhill towards me with her white veil horizontal behind her. She leapt off beside me (dodgy brakes, I thought) and said, 'Welcome to Colchester, I'm Freda' with a broad grin from ear to ear. Well, I thought, if they are all like her it is going to be fine. She showed me to my room and said, 'Tea in the main mess at 4 pm.' In the corridor, as she was leaving, I was introduced to Dorothy, a British Red Cross and St. John's welfare officer who, after showing me where everything was, said she would call and take me over to tea at 4 pm. How kind and welcoming everyone was and it continued to be so for the next sixteen years.

On my first morning, after meeting Matron, I went to

work with a senior captain to get to know the routine and how things were expected to be done – a quiet ward to break me in gently.

There were to be three big surprises compared with civilian nursing and very unexpected they were too. Nurse training schools in the '50s had a very strict hierarchy; one worked happily with middle, senior and staff nurses on duty but in the dining room and socially one only mixed with nurses in one's own preliminary training group of about forty nurses. In the QAs I found that Matron would address one formally as 'Sister' or by rank on the ward but the minute one stepped into the sisters' mess she would usually address you by your Christian name. An even bigger shock was that one was expected to sit next to Matron at table if the next seat was vacant. In those days, in polite society, one would not discuss politics, religion or sex but if something was on the front page of *The Times* or *The Telegraph* regarding subjects that were to be the concern of the army, political or not it would be discussed at the supper table and we were encouraged to join in the conversation with senior officers. What good training it was because as a junior sister one might be asked to look after a brigadier and his wife at a cocktail party or royalty as Princess Margaret was our colonel-in-chief and later to have to speak to Her Majesty the Queen. The animated conversations would go to and fro across the dining table at supper time and were quite memorable at times, amusing and informative. It gave one confidence to speak to a cross-section of all nationalities that one might meet in the coming years.

The next surprise I found was that on days off we had our breakfast in bed on a lovely tray with silver teapot and water jug. We filled in a breakfast book the night before asking for light or full breakfast and requested the time between 8 am and 9.30 am. There was a good reason for this privilege. The ground floor of the mess was like a busy hotel with numerous people passing through: chefs, stewards, stores being delivered, quartermasters checking equipment, visitors, etc. We were expected to be immaculate in turn-out in uniform or mufti – a long mirror was always placed by the front door to check one's appearance before leaving – and who needs that at 8 am on one's day off? This happened everywhere in the world except on acute active service or where curfews were in operation and civilian staff couldn't get in.

The last surprise would be the result of the classification of Dangerously Ill Listed (DIL) and Seriously Ill Listed (SIL) for patients. Next of kin were flown out to be at the bedside immediately, anywhere in the world, and it also gave permission to order extras over and above the standard food rations if sanctioned by the medical officer overseeing the ward. (It was usually, 'Sign here please or you don't get your morning coffee, sir!' No one ever refused!)

Fresh milk was not readily available overseas so evaporated milk diluted was used instead but fresh milk could be obtained for very sick soldiers even if it had to be flown in. A severe burns case flown in from Thailand was in my ward and demanded steak and chips every day and got it for many weeks. Several times I have ordered a bottle of Champagne for severely injured soldiers with multiple gunshot wounds who were finding that food tasted like sawdust. It would come up with the rations, go to chill in the fridge until 11.45 am or 5.45 pm when I would set a small tray with a Champagne flute (from QM stores) and pour out at the bedside to the soldier's astonishment. Suddenly the rest of the ward would be round the bed saying, 'Give us a sip.' It was a boost to the morale as much as to stimulate the appetite before meals, which I found very successful at times – who doesn't like a bit of spoiling? I found the QAs full of good ideas and common sense, no one had time for nitpicking and we had a very professional and comfortable working environment, which one didn't really appreciate until one had left.

Three weeks on day duty then my first three weeks night duty. I remember the lovely matron giving me the report and saying if I had a problem in the night I wasn't to hesitate to call her! No matron had ever said that to me before but later on I was to understand why. We had two night sisters, one on the general side and one on maternity and we were allowed to have dinner together in their offices at 1 am and tea at 4 am. I was the only trained nurse on for all the general wards with only National Service Royal Army Medical Corps (RAMC) orderlies Class III, who were not allowed to give injections. I was responsible for every drug, injection and treatment given. Many penicillin injections were three-hourly then so I kept slim running up and down stairs most of the night. Having trained at a highly specialised research hospital I had never nursed a simple hernia, appendix or orthopaedics. Trauma surgery was quite new to me and was to become a large part of my working life in the QAs. Colchester Garrison held one of the only two military prisons and took the lesser of the serious charges. The more serious charges of murder, rape and grievous bodily harm went to Shepton Mallet – now closed. Colchester Military Corrective Establishment (MCE) better known to others as 'The Glass House' had their own sick bay but if it was suspected an operation might be required patients were sent to us. Strict rules and regulations were applied. If my memory serves me right patients were asked to sign a form saying they would not try to escape or they would have a 24-hour guard with them, which was a nuisance for everyone. No outdoor clothes were allowed, only pyjamas and 'hospital blue' dressing gowns and plimsolls. Known as SUS patients (soldiers under sentence) they only left the ward under RAMC escort to attend X-ray, etc. Checks were made at irregular intervals day and night by the orderly sergeant of the day and details noted.

A rather small-in-stature SUS from the MCE led us quite a dance over a number of weeks. I came across him first when I was overseeing the surgical ward one afternoon. He had a history of swallowing razor blades and broken light bulbs in the hope of having an operation and some convalescence. Nothing was seen on X-ray and after a couple of days he returned to the MCE. The second time I came across him was in the next ward up the corridor, orthopaedics, where he had persuaded some doctor he had a slipped disc. (A very good actor this one and I wondered if he took it up professionally after leaving the army.) He stayed for a few days and was returned to the MCE once more. I next met him on the ENT ward on night duty – he had worked his way up the corridor by this time, also towards the nearest exit point.

I had a good look at his throat and it really was nasty and raw and he was on penicillin. All went well for five nights. When I entered the ward at 6 am to collect temperatures for Matron's report on my final round, his bed was empty but made immaculately. He could have passed a nursing practical exam with full marks. I was assured by the orderly he had just gone to the bathroom; I told him to keep an eye on him and phone me if there was a problem. I continued on upstairs and at the second ward suddenly all the telephones on the floor began to ring. I dashed to a phone. 'Please come, he's gone,' said the frightened orderly. I ran.

During the week he had quietly stolen trousers, jacket, shoes and shirt from various bed patients' wardrobes and had hidden them in a large metal linen bin in the bathroom. He had jammed the bin up against the door, gone through a small window, escaped across Abbey Field down to the railway station and had caught the 6.25 am to London. He was found a week later in Bournemouth. ('Gone for convalescence,' said a lady WI member.) I wasn't sure if losing an SUS was a court-martial offence but luckily all checks had been carried out and I was exonerated from any blame — I breathed a sigh of relief. This experience with SUS patients would prove very useful to me in Germany six years later.

One evening on night duty the maid arrived with my breakfast tray as usual at 6 pm saying not to go to Matron's flat for report but to proceed to the hospital and Matron would give me the report in her office. There was 'something going on'. Down in the mess the bush telegraph reported a ten-tonne soft-top truck had overturned on a very wet road. It was full of soldiers and many had been brought in with head injuries. A soft-top truck offers little protection and injuries could be severe. In Birmingham we had 'The Accident Hospital' so I had never been involved with 'casualties' as such. It was going to be an interesting night.

About thirty soldiers were in the process of being admitted, X-rayed, cross-matched for blood and preparation if necessary for going through the operating theatre. Matron had already arranged for a Sgt RAMC SRN to look after the rest of the hospital and the ten most seriously injured were being admitted to the surgical ward, where I was to stay all night. No chaos, just staff and doctors quietly going about their tasks, Day Sister helping me to admit and settle in bed the serious cases — all had been in full kit: battle dress, boots and gaiters. Some wag said they were all going to a dance! All were on quarter hourly pulse and blood pressure all night so we could react quickly if cerebral haemorrhage occurred.

By 11.30 pm all had been admitted, blood drips proceeding normally, observations all up to date, day staff gone off duty and by midnight all were asleep and snoring, the only sound in the ward. I was impressed. The night proceeded without further incident and all made uneventful recoveries over the next few weeks. They were from the King's Regiment Liverpool so there was a great deal of humour in that ward.

Many years later, after I was married, my husband taped a Radio 4 programme, 'Not all blood and bandages', which featured interviews from wartime QAs, one of whom was Col. Ursula Dowling, our matron at Colchester. She had been responsible for a 1,200-bedded tented hospital complete with facilities for X-ray, operating theatre, laboratory, sterilizing unit, etc. taken over after D-Day and used as the fighting units moved forward. This was regularly put up in forty-eight hours, ready to receive casualties and when directed taken down, packed away in forty-eight hours, moved twenty to fifty miles or so up the road and erected again. An outstanding exercise to me now but routine in wartime.

In 1956 two important things happened. The first custom-built QA officers' mess in the UK was opened in the spring. It was lovely with spacious bedsitting rooms for all, and flats for matrons. The ground floor divided by sliding doors into ante-room, dining room, visitors' room, etc. and could be opened the full length of the building for formal occasions.

An opening ball was held and we had a most wonderful evening. Generals, brigadiers, colonels, etc. were resplendent in scarlet mess dress and ladies were in ball gowns. As very junior officers, some of us had gone out to buy our first ball gown, very anxious not to let the side down. We assembled early for Matron to tell us the format for the evening. Her eyes travelled along the line and, smiling, she congratulated us on our appearance and said we were a credit to the QAs, which reassured us and we began to relax and enjoy our evening of playing hostess. The buffet supper spread over several tables the width of the dining room and was a revelation to me. Having grown up in the war and rationing only recently finished, I was looking for the first time at whole hams, salmon, enormous turkeys and all the trimmings, luscious puddings and many cheeses I had never seen before. We danced the night away with handsome officers in uniform and it was indeed a night to remember.

Later that year I was asked to help theatre staff with a special task. From quartermaster stores came brand new surgical instruments coated in special grease-like petroleum jelly. We were to clean, check and pack them in special sets. We made cotton wool swabs, cut and prepared dressings and gamgee into certain sizes and separate packs ready for all to be sterilized. We had no idea what it was all in aid of but this was the beginning of preparation for 'Suez' military operation. For weeks and weeks there was a continual hum of green army vehicles of all descriptions going into workshops day and night and later emerging in sand colour with a large 'H' on the top of every vehicle. We had fun trying to suggest what it might stand for but we never did get it right. Suddenly all the boyfriends from the signals officers' mess disappeared overnight and that was it. We knew when the news said they had landed in Port Said. Luckily fighting only lasted about five days so we did not have many casualties.

By a strange coincidence, three years later I was at the hospital in Aldershot on a theatre sisters course when all the Suez supplies were returned in their original packs and crates. They had been hanging around somewhere on the quayside in Port Said where rats and other nasties still run around over and under everything there – a pretty filthy area. The laboratory tested all the supplies and found no contamination had occurred. I was impressed with the army system, as it obviously worked.

The next new QA to arrive in the mess was Joyce, a midwife, which was nice as we could be on night duty together. One night on my way to maternity for dinner, passing the orthopaedic ward I could hear voices, unusual at 1 am. I went in. 'The babies are being born with their boots on tonight, Sister.' I smiled at the thought. The ward above was post natal and was usually quiet, as the routine was not to disturb the new mums between 11 pm and 5 am, when the babies went out again to feed. Any fretful baby was looked after by the nursery nurse giving mum a good night's rest. It was a very old hospital and the floors and doors did creak. Someone had been walking up and down and disturbing the boys. I told the orderly to make tea for those awake and to settle them down again. On arriving I asked Joyce if there had been a problem in the ward. In those days mums were not allowed up and all had a bell to call. No one had called. Joyce immediately went to check but found nothing amiss.

Nothing was mentioned again until breakfast. Sitting alongside three senior majors behind newspapers, we exchanged greetings and asked if all was quiet. I asked Joyce if anyone had spoken about last night. 'Well, it was a bit odd,' she said. 'One mum said she had seen me in my long cloak doing a round and then disappearing into the bathroom!'

'Sounds like the grey lady,' said a voice behind a newspaper. 'The hospital ghost, an old QA who usually appears three days before an unexpected death.'

Joyce and I looked at each other, trying not to show our disbelief. The majors disappeared on duty for 8 am.

Three days later, a Saturday night, I went to Matron for the report and she said, 'A sad case, we lost a soldier this afternoon. He had a subarachnoid haemorrhage playing football and died instantly.'

Similar incidents happened twice more during my time at Colchester and the anaesthetist, Stephen, said he had seen the apparition on the top corridor disappearing into a ward and was told by the colonel it would be the grey lady.

Stephen, a national service anaesthetist, was also responsible for introducing me to more good food. He was newly married and his wife, Marjorie, used to come up from London for the occasional party or dance. When Stephen was on weekend call he was allowed to go into town for a meal as long as he could be contacted. He kindly invited me to join him to eat at The George and The Red Lion. Both were old coaching inns in the old Roman town. I had never been in such salubrious places before and I will never forget being invited to try Lobster Thermidor – absolutely delicious. Many years later my husband suggested it when we were out celebrating his birthday with relatives and I turned it down because I considered it much too expensive at £2 10s. What a fool I was. Our families remain good friends and we still enjoy good food together after nearly fifty years.

A steep learning curve in military discipline presented itself to me on night duty as a very junior sister. We had no responsibility for the hospital reception, it was run by a day or night wardmaster and we rarely entered. A single door opened into the main hospital corridor and occasionally after the sisters' mess was locked at 11 pm Matron would return from a social engagement via reception and enter the corridor to return to the mess. One could always see the lights on underneath the door, particularly after I had turned off all the corridor lights at 11 pm. One night it appeared to be in darkness, which concerned me as any high-ranking officer could walk into reception without notice. I decided to investigate. I walked through the dark and empty area following a distant very dim light off to the right and came across a small cubbyhole containing a camp bed with the night wardmaster fast asleep and dead to the world. Underneath the bed were his shoes neatly placed – this showed 'intent'.

I stood for a time, expecting him to wake, but he never stirred. I knew what I should do but I felt I needed confirmation so I went up to maternity where Freda, a captain, was in charge. Yes, I had to go down, wake him and say I was going to put him on 'charge' in the morning. All the way back I was hoping and praying that he was up on his feet so I could reprimand him and tell him to make a strong cup of tea. No such luck, he was still dead to the world. So I had to do my duty. At about 6 am he came round to apologise and suggested I forget about the charge. Sorry, I had to say, a senior officer also knew so it had to go ahead.

Telling Matron wasn't a problem but I also had to report and make a statement to the regimental sergeant major – a traditional type, large, fearsome, waxed moustache and boots you could see your face in. I approached him with some apprehension. 'Well, Sister,' he started – I held my breath – 'thank you, I've been trying to catch this young man for many weeks because he's not been doing the night cleaning duties properly.' I breathed a sigh of relief, left the statement and departed. Phew!

The next day an orderly told me quietly that the night wardmaster was cleaning out the pig bins and had lost both stripes but within weeks he had one stripe back on his arm and shortly afterwards the second stripe was up, so I felt better about the whole thing. Nearing Christmas we had an all ranks dance when all sisters had to appear in No 1 uniform – not ideal to dance in. The night corporal was in a huddle with his mates and I had a feeling they were daring him to ask me to dance. He did and this good-looking young man was a very good dancer and I thoroughly enjoyed it and thanked him. Fortunately I never had to put a soldier on a charge again.

That Christmas I was able to use my ENT knowledge and make a soldier's Christmas Day a little better. Only a few wards were open, as most patients had been sent home. I was overlooking ENT and found a rather poorly older sergeant with a severe middle ear infection, in pain and completely deaf in both ears. On inspection I found the other ear packed with wax. He said he had been deaf in that ear for about ten years! How this had escaped two annual medical inspections I do not know. I asked the MO's permission to treat it and he agreed. I used an old method of warm saturated solution of soda bicarbonate, which I still find the best method I have been taught. It shrinks the wax gently separating it from the wall of the external ear in a way the oil doesn't always do. It took about one and a half hours of repeated applications, but eventually it was ready to syringe using a very gentle method. This again took several goes but rocks and rocks of wax came out – as he said, 'Enough to make a rockery, Sister.' It was rewarding to leave him able at least to hear television or the radio on his headphones for Christmas Day. Administering painkillers for one ear and soothing wax drops for the sore lining of the other ear, I returned late for lunch and had to apologise to Matron and explain. One of the few times that 'shop' was discussed at the lunch table.

Although I didn't realise it at the time, I was coming to the end of my introduction to army nursing at Colchester. Thanks to an excellent matron, who had now moved on, I was gaining confidence from support given to me in disciplinary and nursing decisions I had taken. I had worked on every ward in the hospital, bringing me up to date with medical procedures I hadn't used since training days. I had thoroughly enjoyed all the social occasions and as 'bar member' I had been taught how to organise a cocktail party for 250 guests without having sleepless nights. I had also considerably increased my appreciation of good food.

Before I leave Colchester I have a confession to make: as a very junior sister I refused to carry out a 'lawful written command' and was never found out. We had quite a few patients coming in suffering from kidney stones, a very painful condition. It often affected WWII soldiers who had served in North Africa in the El Alamein campaign where there was a shortage of drinking water. To confirm the diagnosis one had to have a special kidney X-ray known as an intravenous pyelogram or IVP. The patients arrived in time for supper Tuesday to be prepared for IVP Thursday pm. The problem was that if any gas was trapped in the intestines it could obliterate the kidneys. The X-ray had then to be repeated the next week, which was a nuisance for everyone concerned and the patient in particular.

The two-day preparation to try and avoid this was 1 oz of castor oil at 7 pm Tuesday followed by cascara tablets on the Wednesday evening. I had very bad memories of small amounts of castor oil in my childhood, as my father was a great believer in its properties; this came from being in the trenches of WWI. When soldiers went down with dysentery the loss of fluids was severe and he told me that they would be given a *cupful* of castor oil to drink, which sounds horrendous but played its part in their recovery. It produced a coating of oil in the intestines, which eased the pain and general soreness, but it also put back a lot of calories, which had been lost.

One Tuesday evening I was on duty and just finishing giving out supper, which often had prunes and custard for pudding. Where my words came from I don't know to this day, but peering down into the container of prune juice syrup I said, 'Sergeants for IVP Thursday, one ounce of castor oil or a cupful of prune juice?'

'Cup of prune juice please, Sister,' came the chorus from the three soldiers.

I then realised what I had done but decided I would not retract but would accept the consequences if it didn't work and I knew that castor oil did not always work. I had an uneasy forty-eight hours. Thursday pm came and the three went off to X-ray having only had a light breakfast at 6 am that day. I was a very worried sister.

At 2.40 pm there was a knock on my office door. 'I'm back, Sister.'

'Er, everything alright, Sergeant?'

'Fine, Sister.' Sigh of relief from me.

At 3 pm another knock on my door. 'I'm back, Sister.'

'Er, everything alright, Sergeant?'

'Fine, Sister.'

At 3.20 pm a knock on my door. 'I'm back, Sister.'

'Everything alright, Sergeant?'

'Fine, Sister.'

It had worked. Never again did I give out castor oil for IVP when I was on duty. I never asked a nurse or orderly to give prune juice and it was never put on the report but what my staff did in my absence I never asked. Many years later when I was at Iserlohn a Canadian surgeon came in and threw a packet of pills onto my desk. 'Next IVPs try these, Sister.'

'Oh, and what is different about these than all the other purgatives?'

'Well it's strange, they are a derivative of prunes!'

I started to laugh and it was hard to stop – he really thought I'd gone mad and stared at me. 'I've news for you,' I said. 'I've been giving my IVPs prune juice for the last six years and I've never had a failure yet!' I never knew if he believed me but after that I never saw castor oil on the instructions again. I was to come across castor oil as a treatment in another situation in Ghana when a young woman nearly died of Blackwater fever, but I had kept the service's Eleventh Commandment: 'Thou shall not get found out' in the first instance of refusing to obey a lawful command.

5

Ghana

May 1957 – November 1958

After eighteen months at Colchester and enjoying the life, I was invited to extend my short service Commission from two years to four years, which I did. Shortly afterwards I was sent for by Matron and asked if I was interested in going to Ghana as a relief theatre sister. The sister concerned had had her appendix out when she had in fact got infective hepatitis with referred pain in the appendix region, consequently she was very ill. Army personnel will say never volunteer for anything but in this case one had to if one wished to go. Matron suggested I discuss it with my parents and come back and tell her in the morning.

In March 1957 the Gold Coast – or 'white man's grave' as it was known – had gained its independence and become Ghana. We still had a very active military hospital in Accra looking after the Ghanaian Army and later the police as well. Our staff was mainly Ghanaian apart from the sisters, doctors and a few senior NCOs in stores, radiography and pharmacy. Over the next few years we would be training new sisters how to run a military hospital and eventually hand over completely.

British staff were seconded and the Ghanaian government paid our wages, transit and a small gratuity after eighteen months or three years service.

Looking back, I had joined the QAs having only worked in an ENT theatre as staff nurse/acting sister for one year. Apart from being an observer for a morning in general theatre I had not even removed an appendix, hernia or varicose veins, far less seen orthopaedics. It never crossed my mind I might have to assist with craniotomies (brain operations), Caesarean sections and all the rest – would I cope with it all?

There was a common attitude with many wartime experienced matrons that we were all competent and could tackle anything thrown at us and consequently one did!

Father thought it might be a good time to go and said that was what I had joined for 'so go for it, gal.'

Instructions regarding clothes to take were absolute; nothing but cotton was acceptable in the pretty awful climate. Temperatures ranged from 80 to 90°F on the coast or 130°F upcountry. Humidity of 80 to 90% made it most trying.

First stop Marks & Spencer's to buy four sets of cotton

undies – underslips had to be cotton too. One was excused stockings as one couldn't get them on wet legs! Grey ankle socks were acceptable with duty shoes.

In 1957 it was impossible to buy cotton dresses anywhere in winter except at one shop, Hunts of Bond Street, where they catered for ladies who cruised all year round. Dresses had to be sleeveless and collarless, hang in an 'A' line from the shoulders, and no waist bands or belts which could trigger off prickly heat – a scourge of the tropics. Air had to be able to circulate – no narrow skirts.

Never before or since have I been out to buy eight dresses in one afternoon. What excitement! I took a friend with me to give me moral support. Four everyday shopping dresses at £3 10s each. Four best dresses for dances and parties, etc. Very pretty cottons in vivid colours ideal for the tropics £6 to £8 each. One stole for air-conditioned places. A very good buy, they all lasted and looked well even though they were laundered every time they were worn. Good Lancashire cotton!

I had never flown before and was naturally apprehensive travelling alone. The BOAC Stratocruiser was enormous and twin decked. On the lower deck was a bar reached by a tight spiral staircase. I had twin seats to myself at the rear of the plane with plenty of room to spread out and later to sleep. I had delicious salmon for supper and a very kindly, attentive male steward looked after me the whole journey – those were the days. We stopped at Rome before settling for the night and came down at Kano, northern Nigeria, as dawn was breaking and I saw my first camel being led past the airport block.

The final descent into Accra in Ghana was like coming down into a different world. My hometown of Sheffield in wartime and post-war was a very dark, grey place. The Clean Air Act had only just come in and the industrial area was very black compared with Derbyshire a few miles away. The rain forests surrounding Accra were such a vivid green, having the highest rainfall in the country. The earth was red laterite and would become red mud when it rained – wellies and an umbrella were essential at such times. The new university at Achimota gleamed in the sunlight, a very new one-storey red-brick compound. The beautiful tulip trees with deep red flowers were peeping out from the tops as we descended. All birds would turn out to be in parrot colours, bright red and yellow; bee-eaters, blue kingfishers, black vultures with bare head and neck. It was as though I had been dropped into Technicolor.

I stepped out of the plane and into a sauna of very warm humid air, which would remain with me for the next eighteen months. One was to be constantly wet and perspiration ran down one's back, one's legs and into one's shoes, off one's chin onto letters or ward reports or whatever document one was reading or completing (the ink would run – no biros then), and it would take three months to get acclimatised so that it didn't bother one too much. One learned to apply make-up to damp faces very quickly.

After a warm welcome from the sisters in the mess, I was shown to my room, one in a long row of single-storey accommodation complete with mosquito nets, shutters to keep out the rain and a small light in the base of the wardrobe to stop mildew growing on shoes and clothes. Bed linen and pillows never smelled fresh, always fusty, but one got used to it. I ate a good breakfast and then was ready for bed after a warm bath. The ablutions, as they are known in the army, were at the end of the verandah, loos and cubicles containing old-fashioned Victorian baths on curved legs. On my way to the bath a sister put her head out of a window. 'Don't forget to look under the bath for snakes, Margaret.' Hells teeth! They hadn't told me anything about creepy crawlies. I approached the large bath with care and trepidation and bent down: all clear. I turned on the cold tap as instructed because the water coming out was warm enough to bath in. I leaned back and closed my eyes; bliss, five minutes and I'd be in my bed, marvellous. I opened my eyes and there sitting on the bath between the taps was a very large emerald green stick insect. Would it sting? Bite? Was it lethal? A triangular shaped head seemed to have two bulbous eyes on stalks which peered round independently of each other. The 'thing' seemed to be sitting on its haunches and boxing with its front legs. I moved fast, grabbed a towel and shot up the verandah calling to the sister: 'There's something nasty in the bathroom.' She had no idea what it could be and I was hoping it would still be there or she would think I'd 'gone bush' and I'd only just arrived. It was. She looked and then started to laugh and laugh. When she stopped she said, 'You're alright, Margaret, it's a large praying mantis and it only eats its mate after mating!' What a relief.

That night I had many strange creatures in my room but felt relatively safe inside my mosquito net. The geckos, little transparent lizards that ran up and down the walls eating the flies and small nasties, were silent until one made a disparaging remark about someone in the mess when a mixture between a chuckle and a tut tut seemed to emerge from them. Flying insects the size of wasps, which fluttered round the lights in the wet season, dropped their wings and died leaving bodies all over the floor. As a little girl I was rather afraid of moths and suddenly sitting on the top of the mosquito net pole was the most beautiful moth in autumn colours of stone, burnt orange and browns, the size of a dinner plate – I was never worried by moths again. There were also small lizards and in the wet season toads were often visitors to our rooms. The hum of mosquitoes sent us to sleep.

We had 48 hours stand down to get over jet lag so two days later I reported to the operating theatre to start taking over from Yvonne, who had taken over with only six weeks' experience as a student nurse! She is still a good friend. We ran a clinic for families to have dressings done, as wounds were difficult to heal in the high humidity; minor injuries went septic very quickly. One of my patients was a small boy of three and a half years with a septic thumb. He was with Mum, clutching a teddy bear with his left arm and there sitting between the ears was a large green praying mantis! It was called Peter and was a pet, which lived on the curtains at home. Every morning it arrived on teddy. One morning it was missing and the little boy was very upset – Mum whispered that it could have died. Two more days went by and then it was back, great excitement. The little boy looked up at me with a broad grin on his face: 'My Daddy says Peter's got a smile on his face.' Staff and patients dissolved into laughter but I had to say very seriously, 'Then I think you will have to rename Peter because I think he's a girl!'

In that first week in Accra I was introduced to George, headmaster of the Army School; he was in his forties and lived in 'A' Mess in Gifford Camp, the main HQ of the garrison. He was kind and helpful to all the sisters, particularly those without transport for social occasions.

George had been an RAF photographic interpreter at the Allied Intelligence Unit at Medmenham in the war and one of the first to handle a new photograph of Peenemunde on the Baltic showing the launch site of a VI rocket – a 'doodlebug' as they were known. He is mentioned in Flight Officer Babbingnton Smith's book *Evidence in Camera*. He was a superb photographer himself and an ornithologist and did work for the British Museum sending back rare specimens of birds' eggs.

With George as chaperone several of us were able to visit places of interest difficult without a companion who knew the customs of the country. Some years later George married Daphne, the girl I had gone out to relieve and sadly he died in 2003 aged ninety-three.

The women of Ghana wore 'mammy cloths' – high quality Lancashire cotton for export only, beautiful bright colours often in large repeating patterns sold in a length as a sari. It was made up into a wrap-around long skirt with a cropped top giving a cool gap between top and bottom. The clothes always seemed to retain their bright colours no matter how many times they were washed. Many sisters brought back to the UK a favourite pattern to have made up here. In the bottom of my trunk I still have a lilac and white party dress made up by Madam Maria, a French couturiere whom we patronised as a special treat when we had cash to spare. She was a great character, greeting us with 'Hello darlings' in a husky voice. Her strapless dresses were beautifully, lightly boned which never let one down!

Up in northern Ghana, where it was so hot the cropped top would be discarded, many mammies went bare-breasted with a sling of cloth to secure the piccin who continued to breast feed and sleep while mammy worked. They were beautiful babies, contented with big brown eyes; they in turn thought our blonde haired and blue-eyed babies were fascinating.

On one of our trips north we visited Kumasi, Tamele and Bolgatanga, which was almost on the border of French Togoland. Bolgatanga had a large and very interesting market, which George wanted us to see. As we approached on foot we could hear the cacophony of sound issuing forth from the mammies who ran the entire market. The noise was incredible as different stalls cried their wares. This was Ghanaian women's liberation at its best. They were in charge of hiring and firing the men who helped them, bought or bartered their wares and one could hear the harangue going on about the quality of the produce – a wide variety of vegetables, large and small gourds of green, yellow, orange and reds, and colourful spices of all varieties. The only blot on the landscape was the fresh fish and meat stalls, *black* with flies from which I averted my eyes. Women carrying very heavy loads on their heads always walked several paces behind the men, who often carried nothing and sure enough when the market was over they were once more in their place a few paces behind their men. Ghanaian and Nigerian men and women had a great sense of humour and if you made them laugh you could be their friend for life.

Transport for many working people was in open-topped lorries, which hurtled down the centre of the road and terrified me when George was teaching me to drive. He kept asking why I was stopping the car at the side of the road! I learned quickly how to do a 'racing change' of gears going up steep escarpments on my lessons and it was nothing to do fifty miles in the afternoon. Many nasty accidents occurred with these lorries full of people and they had little or no protection if there was an accident. They carried unusual slogans or names on the front and I have a photograph of one in a ditch on its side with 'Say what you like' on the front!

One of my more 'hairy' moments came on night duty. On taking report I was told there was a soldier lodging for the night only in the small four-bedded isolation ward used for any very infectious cases such as cholera, etc. It was self-contained with its own bathroom. I was told that the patient was on his way to the mental hospital in Accra. He had had his medication and the orderly sergeant would see to him in the morning. The door was locked and I had nothing to do with him.

At about 11 pm when everyone was settled down there was a terrible noise coming from his ward: breaking crockery, splintering of wood, etc. It could be heard all over the compound. I telephoned the duty doctor who happened to be the medical specialist and he instructed me to send a runner over for a prescription for 10 cc of paraldehyde to be given intramuscularly. It was a highly efficient psychiatric drug (not used now) but not pleasant to give. A large syringe and a large wide-bore needle were required as it was rather sticky like streptomycin. It hurts as it goes into the muscle and there is an unpleasant smell rather like formaldehyde, which is excreted later through the breath and pores of the skin. By now this terrible noise had been going on for at least twenty-five minutes, keeping everyone awake. Thinking about the possibility of having help around if anything went wrong, I briefed two of the night guards patrolling the camp. I explained to them that if I was attacked they were to get me out and inform the medical officer. They seemed to understand and I approached the door, unlocked it and entered to a scene of utter devastation. He had smashed everything within sight including the washbasin and had used sharp pieces of it to smash the wooden surround of the bedsprings – the mattress and sheets were in shreds. I turned to speak to the guards – gone! They were running away as fast as their legs would carry them. I was now getting cross because they had decided it could be contagious and they could also 'go bush'.

I approached the young man who was starkers and glistening all over with sweat as though he had been oiled, and he must have been exhausted in the heat. I put on my no-nonsense voice: 'Now come along, you have wakened the entire hospital and you must stop this noise, now lie down on the mattress and turn over on your left side and I'll give you an injection to make you sleep.' And he did!!! With some trepidation I knelt down on the floor beside him, cleaned the correct part of the buttock and slowly injected this painful syringe of paraldehyde. He never moved, thank goodness, as he could easily have snapped my neck if he had wished to. I covered him with the remnants of the sheets and, bidding him goodnight, escaped. My heart was going like the clappers and I made my way over to sister's office on maternity saying, 'Open the drug cupboard and get out the medicinal brandy because I need a drink.' I sat and sipped the tot telling her what had happened. We never heard another sound out of the ward and he was transferred to another hospital in the morning.

Some time before Christmas, Matron had asked me to

take over the job of messing officer. She should have enquired into my qualifications for the job but she didn't. I had grown up in the War and Mum would not teach my sister or me how to cook – she didn't fancy either of us wasting any of the precious rations. We both married without having done much cooking although I could do a good scrambled egg from my invalid cookery course in nurse training.

Throughout my time on the wards in the army, I was able to prepare crustless bread and butter and fluffy scrambled eggs for the very first meal for soldiers post-gastrectomy who had just had that awful gastric tube removed forty-eight hours post op. If they enjoyed their first meal for afternoon tea they usually coped with a light gastric diet with no problems. We always seemed to have bread, butter, eggs, milk and cheese in our kitchens from 'subsistence' diet rations for soldiers admitted too late in the day for full rations, and if a soldier missed a meal for some test or X-rays, etc. he would always be able to go to the ward kitchen for something to eat. Another sensible arrangement.

One advantage I had as messing officer was that I enjoyed good food. Christmas Day came and as usual I reported to Matron at 8 am with the menu of the day.

'Good morning, Ma'am, Happy Christmas.'

'Happy Christmas, Margaret, have you defrosted the turkey?'

Pause, what does she mean? 'Pardon, Ma'am?'

She repeated the question. In all honesty I did not understand what she was talking about. At home our turkey would arrive two days before Christmas and as far as I knew the giblets were removed and it was stuffed and went in the oven. I knew the 16-20 lb turkey had arrived from the cold store in Accra but I didn't know it was frozen solid. Matron was obviously rather embarrassed by the ignorant sister and dismissed me smartly to 'sort it out'. I remember muttering 'Well, it's as hot as hell outside' and proceeded to the kitchen. Once more my time as a Girl Guide came to the rescue. I decided the only way was to make a meat-safe, which in the days before portable fridges was attached to a rope and hung high in a tree where the breeze kept it cool at summer camps. I managed to get stockinette (used to protect arms and legs before plaster of Paris is applied) to cover the bird and protect it from flies and creepy crawlies. There was a suitable mango tree outside the kitchen door and we were able to throw a rope over one of the higher branches and raise a platform with the bird on it. Word went around on bush telegraph that there was 'good chop' in the tree and I had to put a cook to sit on the kitchen steps guarding it with his rifle across his lap (I never asked if it was loaded, I didn't want to know). The guard was changed every hour. It dripped and dripped and by about 11 am I managed to get the giblets out and by 1.30 pm I reckoned it was ready to go in the wood fired stove in the kitchen, and at 8 o'clock that night we had our Christmas dinner and very good it was too. The subject was never mentioned by Matron again.

Visiting Yvonne many years later I said, 'Wasn't it funny about the Christmas turkey?'

'What Christmas turkey?'

Matron obviously hadn't told anyone and I hadn't, so no one knew. What a pity; they could all have had a good laugh.

Kwame Nkrumah was the president of newly independent Ghana and although in the first year there was democracy for many years after that it became a dictatorship and things began to get a bit hairy. Opposition members began to disappear, the odd body would be found on the hospital compound – usually in the monsoon drains.

One night I was called to the operating theatre; an African had been nearly hacked to death with a machete. We struggled for a long time to staunch the bleeding and keep him alive but it was a losing battle and a particularly awful job for the anaesthetist who had the worst part of it. The patient died on the table and the anaesthetist left the theatre to be sick in the bushes. I and my Ghanaian staff took a deep breath and started to clear up the slaughterhouse together, we never did find out who the poor man was.

During the second year of my tour we found we had to admit the president several times, when suffering from exhaustion, as he declined to go to the local hospital in case of assassination attempts on his life. He was an Oxford graduate and spoke perfect English whereas we had been speaking pidgin English for over a year. One had to be very careful not to insult him by slipping into the vernacular. If he took a dislike to you, you would hear on the 8 am news that you were being deported on the BOAC plane coming in at 3.20 pm that day. The wives and children were given two weeks to pack, close the house up and leave. This was no idle threat, our own general was asked to leave in this manner. When in conversation I tried to stick to the birds, flowers and fauna of the area and make my escape as soon as reasonable.

Another difficult situation to deal with came when I was still messing officer. I'd gone on duty at 1 pm and just before 2 pm I realised I'd forgotten to put something out for the sandwiches for teatime. It was, of course, siesta time and even the orderlies would sit on the floor, the coolest place, with backs to the wall with their heads on their knees fast asleep. It was the hottest time of the day. I made my way over towards the back door of the kitchen by the mango tree. The mess was a single-storey building with a main ante-room, dining room, cloakrooms and kitchen – completely separate from the living quarters. As I approached I could hear a heated argument going on in the kitchen; I stood in the doorway and saw No.1 cook and No.2 cook screaming at each other, one wielding a carving knife the other a meat cleaver and one getting very close to losing an ear. They never noticed me and their voices rose higher and higher. Visions of my machete man made me realise I had to try to defuse the situation somehow. I edged nearer but not too near in case they turned on me. Making quacking movements with my right hand I said in a very loud voice: 'Yap yap yap yap yap, just like the mammies in Bolgatanga market.' They stopped and turned to look at me. I smiled. Their hands came down and they both started to laugh and they laughed and laughed, almost crying with laughter. I suggested they put the knives down and I would go and get something out of the store cupboard for tea and breathing a sigh of relief I returned to officers ward. Later I found out the row was about No.2 cook stealing more sugar than No.1 cook – there was a definite hierarchy in this matter.

Ex-nurses at my talks have asked how I coped with general and orthopaedic operations in the theatre when I had only seen and taken ENT cases. The answer is the same as Yvonne did when she went in to take over with only six weeks' experience as a student nurse – we read it up. The book *Operating Theatre Techniques*, hopefully up-to-date, was in theatre and listed all the instruments and requirements usually used – we also knew our anatomy and physiology in which we had been examined in training. Not so common these days. The Ghanaian technicians would sterilize and set up our trolleys, we scrubbed up and took the case. The checking of the correct number of instruments and swabs at the beginning, middle and end of operations was done meticulously as we had been taught. Two people would sign the operating register to confirm that all was correct before we left the theatre.

Yvonne and I had started off with a young surgeon captain doing National Service so we did fairly routine operations, but when he left a very senior colonel arrived to finish off his service before retirement and the work really expanded. He had been a well-decorated wartime surgeon so had had to cope with everything coming off the battlefield for many years. He was very pleasant to work with and taught us both a lot.

The operating theatre itself was a great culture shock, as it was not air-conditioned. Most civilian and military hospitals had had air-conditioned theatres for many years but this one had somehow escaped. At the top of the four walls was a gap between the wall and the ceiling of about one to two feet, which held a type of wire netting which allowed any type of wind to blow in leaves, mosquitoes, flies or any other debris floating around. We got used to having a sterile sheet or towel handy to throw over the operating table and trolleys if the debris started to come our way and wait until it had all cleared and then discard the towels and get on with the operation. I never remember any cases of infection, as Africans seem to be a very hardy people.

It was very hot and rather unpleasant when gowned and masked and at regular intervals we would call for 'jungle juice' – a large glass of mixed fresh fruit juice. The technician would carefully remove one's mask and holding the glass near would put the straw in one's mouth and you could empty the glass without getting de-sterilised and have to scrub up again. You then carried on with the operation and had at least replaced your fluid loss.

One day the colonel came to me in my office and said he had just come back from the local hospital and found about thirty fractured femur cases which needed treating with Kunchner nails and one or two patients had been there nearly a year being looked after by their families with food but lying on mattresses in a corridor. He asked if I would agree to assist him on one of the free mornings we had and of course I agreed; I too was horrified at his findings. We had a good supply of all sizes of 'K' nails, which are used if the fracture is complicated and can't be healed by simple traction on ropes and pulleys. X-rays are used to gauge the length and width of the nail required, which is hammered down the centre of the broken bone of the femur holding it together in a straight line and wiring can be used to secure any loose fragments back in line to heal.

He chose the cases carefully according to the degree of problems. One morning we might operate on two cases, another complicated one might take up the entire morning. This method had the patient ambulant on crutches fairly quickly and then they could be returned to their own hospital. Orthopaedics can be quite heavy work and particularly in that heat, but over the next few months we cleared them all and gave considerable help to the local community, which was rewarding. The army was always willing to help the local community where possible when abroad and vice versa. In Singapore, a professor from a local hospital came to the BMH to do a heart operation in theatre on a Gurkha's wife before she had to return to Nepal. At Millbank Military Hospital, specialists from the London hospitals would always give their advice on our cases and help with operations if it was something unusual. Blackwater fever was a known killer in this region; all part of West Africa's 'white man's grave' reputation. It was a particularly awful type of malaria which affected the brain and kidneys so you could have signs of cerebral malaria (from which the babies often died) but it also destroyed the kidneys, hence the name when beetroot-coloured urine is passed before they pack up altogether. Towards the end of my tour in 1958 we had a secretary admitted from the Canadian High Commission, twenty-eight years old and very ill. She had previously been in Indo-China with them and had dutifully taken her anti-malaria pills with no problems. When she was sent to Ghana she suddenly decided she wouldn't take them any more and consequently it hit her hard. She was looked after by the sisters night and day.

The biggest problem was maintaining the correct balance of nutrients for life support without overloading the kidneys as they began to deteriorate. This was controlled by daily fluid balance readings and the giving of nutrients and salts by intravenous drips and very limited food and drink by mouth which she fought against anyway. As her condition continued to deteriorate it was decided to try and get her to the UK and an artificial kidney, which were just coming into use. The services only had one, which was held by an RAF hospital in the south of England. On three separate Wednesdays we booked her on British Caledonian Airways, which only came in once a week, but was as near as possible to the RAF hospital, but each Tuesday she became much worse and too ill to move. One time we were fast running out of bottles of dextrose/saline and the nearest and quickest supply was from the University of Kaduna in Nigeria on the local plane, which called at Lagos before Accra. Someone went up to the airport to meet the plane that evening and found to their horror that the box marked clearly 'Urgent supplies for BMH Accra' had been lifted off and newspapers had been put on in their place! We didn't expect her to survive the night but she did and the supplies arrived safely the next morning.

Advice about her treatment was taken from several specialists in tropical medicine worldwide and one treatment used in the old days taken from a text book was castor oil given by gastric tube, which we did when the kidneys packed up completely for several days and no urine was passed at all; and it seemed to be successful as it put in a lot of calories without water. Because of the cerebral oedema, she was a very aggressive patient (as head injuries can be) and we battled away to get treatments done and became exhausted in the heat with little off duty – our normal 'tropicl' off duty of 'off at 1 pm' or 'on at 1 pm to 8.00 m' had gone out of the window weeks earlier. One day the High Commissioner's wife came into the office at tea-time to find two sisters in tears with frustration – we had tried to give her ice-cold jelly to ease her dry mouth and she had spat it out at us! The next day she passed some urine again and slowly but surely started to improve. After six weeks with us she was discharged to the High Commissioner's residence until she was given permission to fly home. Before she left, the residence gave a cocktail party for all the staff involved at BMH and presented the sisters concerned with lovely Waterman fountain pens. I still have mine – the best I have ever used. She returned home for a year's convalescence but whether she would survive in the future without a kidney transplant is unknown.

Early on in our tour Yvonne and I had infective hepatitis A – probably from a dirty glass but we were nursed together for six weeks, which included convalescence at the Miners Resthouse in Takoradi – the port where all our heavy luggage was delivered off the boats. There was only surf at Accra until they built their new port several years later.

Yvonne went a very yellow colour, which exactly matched her yellow dressing gown but I went a terrible grey. Neither of us was made very welcome on families' ward by the senior sister, but perhaps it was because we were not midwives. I think it was many years since she worked on the general side as we were sent a fried breakfast every morning, which was smartly returned, as it was well known that infective hepatitis cases had an aversion to fats and could feel sick at the smell of it. The Ghanaian nurses were very kind and George went out and bought fresh milk to have on our cornflakes instead of diluted evaporated milk on ration.

After two weeks in the acute stage of the illness the medical specialist returned from two weeks leave and apologised for his absence. He suggested we might like to try some Turkish delight! We looked at him in disbelief and George kindly brought in a box. We took a large square each and gingerly took a bite, savouring its flavour and, realising it was moreish, popping in the rest of the square. It really was delicious and the first thing we had enjoyed since we were ill. Within a short time we had finished the box and were asking for more! I have passed on that tip to anyone suffering from jaundice.

When we were well enough to come off bed rest we were moved to an empty maternity ward complete with baby cots at our beds. For commanding officer's inspection we decided we would fill our cots and put them outside our door on the verandah, as was the practice. We heard the colonel coming and as he turned the corner we heard him say, 'Ah, we have two mums.' When he appeared he found he was looking at two teddy bears snugly wrapped in cotton swaddling blankets. He thought it was great fun but sister was not very amused and we departed for Takoradi shortly afterwards.

We had lost a great deal of weight and I can't say either

of us was very sorry to leave Ghana but I would not have missed the experience for anything – one never complained about supplies again! We had trained four new Ghanaian sisters how to run the military administration and they were all well qualified with many UK postgraduate courses to their names. One of them was Margaret Prempeh, the daughter of the King of Ashanti. On the morning I left, escorting a sick warrant officer home on the plane, she came to my room and charmingly thanked me for my friendship and presented me with some Ashanti gold earrings, which I still have. All being well she would be the next matron of the Ghanaian Military Hospital when we all left and I was sure it would be in safe hands.

6

Aldershot

March 1959 – January 1960

I was posted to Cambridge Military Hospital in order to take the second part of the operating theatre course. I had been given Part 1 on posting to Ghana which said I was qualified to work in an operating theatre, but to receive extra pay (three shillings and sixpence a day) for being in charge, I had to obtain Part II. This was a six-month course in a busy designated hospital and included the teaching of Royal Army Medical Corps (RAMC) theatre technicians, nurses for SRN and potential theatre sisters. I don't think the hospital had changed all that much since my father was there in WWI but the theatre block was new, up-to-date, air-conditioned and sheer luxury after Ghana. It was also going to be lovely to be able to hop on a train to London to see a show or shop.

I reported to Matron at 9 am on the first day and after the usual pleasantries she said, 'I would like you to go to Ward 3 and make a film.' Did she really say what I thought she said?

'Pardon, Ma'am?'

'They are making a film for the Central Office of Information on hygiene and they need a technical advisor for the week,' and with that I was dismissed. The film was called 'The Housefly' showing its filthy habits and I was to be in charge of the dysentery ward admitting very sick soldiers, carrying bedpans suitably covered in the correct covers, washing hands and smoothing fevered brows which were covered in drops of glycerine at regular intervals. We were filming a few minutes for five days and the tedium was unbelievable – who would ever want to be a film star? Many years later at a Queen Elizabeth Hospital reunion a member of my PTS (preliminary training school) saw me across the ballroom and with arm outstretched and finger pointing, shouted as she came across, 'I saw you in a film called "The Housefly".' (No 'Hello, Margaret, how are you?') She ran a nursing home in the south of England and her staff had been shown it. Stardom at last!

After doing the usual share of three weeks night duty I was at last sent to the operating theatre for my course. I'd had a fair amount of experience in Ghana but here I was to gain much more. The teaching side I loved, as my training had been so thorough at QEH, we had taught new nurses continually over the four years. We did all specialities here except Caesarean sections which were done at the Military Louise Margaret Maternity Hospital in Aldershot. It was to be Germany before I assisted at my first Caesarean.

One night I had a call about 10 pm to say they needed to do a craniotomy for a serious head injury, a laparotomy for a possible intestinal obstruction and an orthopaedic case and I knew I hadn't seen any of these cases before. I approached the major in charge of theatre to inform her and expected her to accompany me over to the theatre. 'Off you go, Margaret, you'll be fine,' and with that I took a deep breath and went. A very interesting few hours and back to bed about 3.30 am.

After the terrible air disaster at Farnborough Air Show a few years previously, all but emergency surgery was cancelled. As the planes practised and zoomed overhead it was impossible to hear the spoken word and all the instruments rattled on the trolleys until they had passed, so normal lists were impossible. Thankfully we had no casualties from the show and we organised quite a bit of work for the evenings. The year of '59 had a wonderful long summer, which was marvellous and helped to get me acclimatised to the UK again. We played tennis, sunbathed and lived in our cotton dresses again. Weekends off could be spent in London at the Nuffield Club for Junior Officers in Eaton Square for ten shillings and sixpence B&B and we had a very good social life too.

For the first and only time in my life I went to the races. I and another girl I had not met before were invited to go to Newbury races with a mutual officer friend from the Club. He went fairly regularly and studied racing form. We girls got on fine but neither of us knew anything about racing. He decided we would try for the treble tote and each pick a horse. I chose Devon Customer simply because I'd had a holiday in Devon. The other girl did the same, picking at random a name that meant something to her. The officer was pretty disgusted with our choice and said, as a favourite hadn't won so far, he must pick a favourite. Yes! We won the treble tote! It paid for the entire day at the races and we each went home with £5 in our pocket. Happy days. The course was finished and I was to be posted to pastures new – British Army on the Rhine in Germany – and to further my education with the Canadians.

7

Germany

February 1960 – September 1963

Iserlohn was one of several BAOR (British Army of the Rhine) military hospitals in Germany and not far from the industrial Ruhr in North Rhine Westphalia. The hospital was in a pretty setting by a small lake, the Seilersee, with a gently sloping, heavily wooded hillside on the north side. Rumours had it that in the war somewhere on that hillside was one of the baby farms hoping to produce the pure Aryan race.

We shared the hospital with the Royal Canadian Medical Services and the wards were run either by QAs with Royal Army Medical Corps (RAMC) staff or Canadian sisters and their own staff. It was just as well since Canadians ran their wards closer to the American system than ours. The Canadian surgeons had to get used to our hands-on approach and eventually would trust us to make decisions about all sorts of treatments without their supervision.

The hospital, being a converted Panzer barracks, was

not as ideal as the Nightingale Hospitals. The wards were divided into two-bedded, four-bedded and eight-bedded rooms and there were still the empty gun racks built into the corridor walls. In another block was the administration on the ground floor and on the upper two floors our sisters' mess with kitchen, dining room and ante-room. Our sleeping quarters, which were mainly very large bedsitters, were lovely. All windows were double-glazed, which was needed, as the temperature was often -20°C in the winter months.

A new modern building between the wards housed the operating theatres and I reported as the new 'Brit' theatre sister to work alongside two Canadian sisters, Sam and Jesse, both captains (but equivalent to our majors) at least ten years my senior who had both served in Korea in 1951, running operating theatres in Mobile Army Surgical Hospitals (MASH). Looking back it really was like being dropped into the middle of 'M*A*S*H', the film and TV series. All their technicians were regular soldiers and not conscripts to National Service like ours. Staff was plentiful and we seemed to have twice as many staff as we would have in our theatres. They were well paid and very 'laidback' but I found all pleasant to work with. The only problem I had was the different meanings in the English language.

In 1960 we were still using the old-fashioned methods of

sterilizing instruments. (Now we have trays of instruments ready sterile in a large central supply area where they are washed as well.) We collected the instruments unsterile from cupboards and using metal crates lowered them into water sterilizers heated by steam to boiling point and then boiled for at least five minutes. We had a clean 'laying-up room' in which we would prepare trolleys with sterile mackintosh and towels ready to receive the instruments. The instruments were happily boiling away when we went to the office for Sam to give us all the report and instructions for the morning's list. I was introduced to the staff and when we had finished I said to Sam, 'Shall I go and start?'

'Yes please, Maggie.'

Seeing no identification of rank on any of the boys I hadn't a clue to their experience. I said, 'Who is coming with me to the laying-up room?'

They all fell about, for want of a better description. They went hysterical with laughter and even Sam and Jess couldn't speak above the noise. I stood wondering what I had said.

'Sister, that's something in the red-light district to us, we call it the "set up room"!' I had several boys on each arm saying, 'We are all coming to the laying up room with you, sister.' Oh well, it was a good start. They also had different names for some of the instruments, which took me some time to fathom out.

Road traffic accidents in that hospital were a nightmare. I have never seen, before or since, such horrendous facial and skull injuries. Seatbelt laws were not in place then and it seemed that the Canadians were mesmerised by the tree-lined roads after the open highways in Canada. Many had brought over large, fast cars and too much German beer resulted in many going through the windscreens after driving head on into trees. 'The tree walked into the middle of the road, Sister' they used to say. We spent many nights trying to reconstruct faces and scalps but for the brain injuries we could do little and they would go back home as casualties or in the wooden box. The Canadian government was very concerned and started a twelve-point system on licences, which could mean returning to Canada in disgrace.

A two-year posting to Europe was very special for the Canadians and when the sisters had weekends or leave they were off 'doing Europe' – Germany, France, Italy, Switzerland and the UK, etc. They were very kind and hospitable and would never leave with an empty seat in the car. 'Go pack a bag, Maggie!' they would say if I was off duty too on a Friday evening. On one occasion we set off down the Rhine to Wiesbaden American Officers' Club, met thick fog and arrived at 2 am to stay the night. After a short night and an early breakfast we set off again for Munich and the

Oktoberfest. I think it was on for two weeks but we just had two nights. The five enormous beer tents held hundreds of people at long tables and girls dressed in traditional local costume would deliver trays of full beer steins. There was the most delicious smell of roasting chicken, steaks and sausages cooking nearby mingling with the smell of beer and tobacco smoke, which I will never forget. It was very warm and I soon put away a stein of beer! German bands would be playing familiar drinking songs which we all knew and joined in, swaying to 'drink, drink' with steins of beer in our hands bringing back memories of Mario Lanzo in 'The Student Prince'. Later the girls would dance on the tables too when plates had been cleared away. What a night to remember. Strangely in all the time we were there and walking around Munich next morning we never saw anyone drunk or out of control.

We did several visits to Holland, taking in Arnhem and Oosterbeek where the battles in WWII had taken place with such terrible loss of life. The Dutch were so hospitable and kind. One day, marooned in a sea of bicycles in Amsterdam, we asked the way of a cyclist and he smiled and said, 'follow me' and went miles out of his way to put us on the right road. The kindness of everyone was palpable.

One midsummer evening we drove to Cologne and from a bridge over the Rhine watched the annual Rhine in Flames festival. Many miles away in Koblenz they start lighting bright red flares at the base of the beautiful fairy-like castles, which line the banks of the Rhine; the red is reflected in the water and the entire river appears to be on fire, slowly creeping up to Cologne. A superb fireworks display accompanies it and in the darkness is quite a magical spectacle.

We visited Heidelberg, set on the river Neckar and seemingly suspended in a medieval time warp: the ruins of the 14th century castle on the hillside, Germany's oldest university and the pretty old town of medieval alleyways, the old bridge and student taverns, coffee and cakes at a café by the river.

Dorothy, the welfare officer from Colchester, was posted in and later that year we had a lovely holiday in Austria. A leave warrant took us free to Passau on the German/Austrian border, where we took a boat up the Danube to Vienna. In three days we visited the Schönbrunn Palace, the Sunday afternoon dress rehearsal of the beautiful Lippizana horses at the Spanish Riding School and did the shops, which we found very cosmopolitan and rather disappointing.

We set off by train for Salzburg, which was to be our favourite place. We stayed in a lovely hotel by the bridge over the river Salzach and were introduced to what we now know as duvets, which were of an enormous size and depth.

One had to book a bath and pay extra for it. The maid would unlock the bathroom, run the bath and provide large fluffy towels and then the bathroom would be locked again afterwards.

All the scenes from 'The Sound of Music' were close by and we had coffee and cakes in the beautiful squares. We visited Mozart's house and enjoyed browsing in the friendly little old shops by the river. We bought some of the lovely, delicate, old silver cake servers and forks and admired genuine Loden coats and capes.

One night we booked for the famous Puppet Theatre where, to Mozart's 'Eine Kline Nacht Music', we watched beautiful scenes from rural life played out. One scene, particularly memorable, was of a shepherd and shepherdess, dogs and a flock of sheep. The interaction of the dogs trying to round up the sheep was quite hilarious and laughter rang round the little theatre. A wonderful evening we shall never forget.

We treated ourselves to a genuine Weiner Schnitzel in the Keller restaurant of the hotel before getting the night couchette hack to Dortmund and we slept well all night, returning to work refreshed and with happy memories.

After working in theatre for about a year I was sent to take over the main surgical ward, which included orthopaedics. Sam and Jesse were due to return to Canada and a QA major, 'Scottie', was posted in to take charge. She was a wonderful character with war medals upon her tippet and always joined us for any party at home or away. The Canadian parties went on all night and it was not unusual to find a certain sister attempting a Highland Fling on top of the grand piano at 4 am. The noise was reasonably well tolerated by the matrons!

As mentioned before, the wards were not ideal for keeping a good eye on very sick patients. A four-bedded room was used as an emergency ward with double doors fitted to allow orthopaedic beds with Balkan beams attached to go in and out. The four beds all had piped oxygen and suction units attached and we tried to keep at least one bed available for sudden emergencies.

One Sunday morning I came on duty and was told that two sergeants had been admitted from the same accident. They had been out on the town and had turned over a small car. One young man had a nasty leg laceration and possible mild concussion; he sadly had to be discharged from the army, as he was never the same again. The other was listed DIL and his wife had been sent for from UK as he wasn't expected to survive the day and my instructions were to keep him as comfortable as possible and continue with antibiotics, as everything that could be done had been done.

Going into the ward to see him, he brought to mind a

newspaper cartoon where one is bandaged from head to toe with only two eyes, a nose and a mouth visible. He had a broken femur in one leg and broken lower leg on the other with both up in traction with ropes and pulleys over the end of the bed. One arm was broken, the other severely lacerated and heavily bandaged, a fracture to the base of the skull with head lacerations and broken ribs as well as burns to the back when the overturned car dripped battery acid over him as he was trapped for some time. We also suspected a possible fatty embolism from the broken femur, so he might die at any time. His wife arrived that evening and he survived the night. When he had survived forty-eight hours I began to think he had a chance. Talking gently to him when I was treating him I didn't get much conversation other than 'yes' or 'no' but he was definitely getting more than semi-conscious and I found his eyes following me round as I spoke to the patients.

That week the matron-in-chief, Brigadier Cousins, was doing her inspection of BAOR and we were expecting her with the usual retinue of senior officers from HQ on the Friday morning. We were busy getting ready and I told the orderly to keep the double doors closed until I had explained to the brigadier about this man's injuries, rather than relate them at his bedside. Then we went in and she spoke to the other three patients first and then went over to his bed in the corner. Taking his hand in hers she said, 'Tell me what happened, Sergeant.' He turned and looked hard at me, with a half smile on his face, then turned to her. 'Well, Ma'am, Sister did this, I only came in with a cold.' The ward dissolved into laughter and this comment was passed out to the retinue down the corridor. The brigadier said, 'I think he's well on the way to recovery, Sister!' We now knew we had quite a character in the ward.

At 8 am one morning about four weeks later, I was standing at the door of the ward, as the floor was being polished ready for the commanding officer's inspection the next day. All four beds were on one side of the room and I didn't want to walk on the floor while work was going on. My one QA nurse, a pretty Irish girl, was chatting to the sergeant while doing something and had her back to me.

'Did you go to the dance at the NAAFI last night, nurse?' asked the sergeant.

'Yes, of course,' she replied.

'Did you do the twist?' It was all the rage at the time.

'Yes, of course we did the twist.'

'I can do the twist,' says he and immediately pulls himself up on the monkey chain attached to the Balkan beam above the bed. As he did so there was a crack and the femur separated again. His face was a study of expressions, going from puzzlement, surprise, sudden realization and then horror at what he had just done. We were all watching him and I must confess it was funny to see the expressions on his face. When we stopped laughing there was complete silence. All eight of us in that room realised that this was a 'self-inflicted injury', which was a court-martial offence. Shooting oneself in the foot or getting oneself so sun burned that one was not fit for duty also came into this category.

The sergeant had in fact done nothing more than lift himself off the bed in the recognised way, as he would have done to get on a bedpan or allow his bottom sheet to be straightened or changed. I had seen him do it but I had to be very careful how I reported it. I was convinced that the fracture was pretty unstable or it would not have happened in the normal course of moving. I explained that I would have to tell the colonel, as he would have to go for X-ray and theatre with anaesthetic, for manipulation to reduce the fracture again. There were many serious faces in that room as I left. If I reported how it had really happened and it went in his notes, on return to his unit he could have had three stripes taken away with a great loss of pay. I was glad I had been in the ward at the time and I could be 'economical with the truth' with a clear conscience, as I didn't think a bit of harmless fun was to blame. The colonel showed a certain surprise on visiting the patient but accepted the explanation as I was close by at the time and he organised his return to theatre. For Matron's round I explained quietly 'slight problem with bedpans' and she made no comment other than to ask him how he was and what bad luck. The subject was never mentioned again. From then on he continued to have an uneventful recovery. He worked hard with the physiotherapy and at fifteen weeks we arranged for him to go to Hedley Court in Surrey, a marvellous rehabilitation centre for service personnel, where some of the hostages from Beirut had gone to get over their terrible ordeal. It was run by the RAF and if they couldn't get him back to work then no one could. He left with two sticks, walking slowly down the corridor to say goodbye. He had been a great patient and we were quite sorry to see him go.

One Sunday morning weeks later I had been on night duty and was fast asleep when a Canadian sister came into the room and gently shook me awake. 'Quickly, Margaret, put your radio on. There's a record for you on "Two-Way Family Favourites", it's from "the sergeant and boys of room 4 BMH Iserlohn for Captain Madin with many thanks",' and as I pressed the button for the Forces Broadcasting Station out came Trinni Lopez playing 'Let's twist again like we did last summer'. Sadly I couldn't tell her why I was laughing so much but I thanked her very much for waking me.

During my first year in Iserlohn I was sent back to UK

to attend the junior officers' course for three weeks at the Depot at Hindhead. This contained further knowledge and the working of military law regarding the administration of all nurses in training in the QAs. The course was in preparation for the full time job of company commander when one was responsible to the matron for the welfare and discipline for all nurses in the unit.

One had to know how to deal with 'charges' in the orderly room, of minor misdemeanours, usually nothing more than staying out later than 11 pm with or without a late-night pass. One time it was hard to keep my face straight as a nurse who had returned about 2 am elaborated at some length at being snowbound in Menden about fourteen miles away, but I had been at the officers' mess at the same barracks doing Scottish country dancing with a boyfriend who organised it. I was home on very clear roads by 11.30 pm! The punishments available were usually restriction of privileges, which meant no late passes for a week, or whatever.

For thirteen long days in October 1962 there was great fear of a Third World War. The Russian president, Nikita Khrushchev, continued to send nuclear missiles by sea to Cuba, which could then be trained onto the USA. The climax of diplomatic manoeuvring came at the weekend of 28th and 29th when I was on night duty. The Sunday night was very tense and we knew that 300 miles away on the East German border the Russian tanks were lined up ready to roll should war be declared. Many of the patients had their headphones on all night listening for news but with eyes closed so I didn't know if they were asleep or not. At 1 am the Canadian orderly sergeant of the day came to me and said I must be ready to evacuate the hospital if war came. I'd had no instructions so where did he suggest I put them – the car park? 'Be British, don't panic,' I said, which was probably a bit naughty but I felt this was getting slightly ridiculous. Doing a quick round of the hospital before going to tea at 4 am I went into my own ward and a quiet voice in the dark ahead of me said, 'The ships have turned back, Sister.'

'Thank you and thank God,' I said and went to tea to pass on the news. I think the orderlies made an awful lot of cups of tea that night.

In June '63 the QA mess had an invitation to visit the Royal Highland Fusiliers Barracks for HRH Princess Margaret's visit and parade, followed by a strawberries and cream tea on the lawn. Being an afternoon visit it meant only those on days off could go. Matron was a little bit miffed, as apart from herself and a deputy matron only six sisters had been invited and after all she was also our colonel-in-chief. Our instructions were to wear the more comfortable walking out dress No. 2 uniform, as we were not likely to meet anyone. Three Canadians and three QAs were organised to go and it was a lovely afternoon. After the parade we were making our way through a small door in a walled garden to the lawns for our strawberry tea but what we didn't know was that Princess Margaret and her lady-in-waiting were looking down on us from the ladies rest room. 'Those are my nurses and I wish to meet them,' she said. The next thing we knew was an equerry appeared and said to me that Princess Margaret had asked to meet us and would I please organise it quickly.

Small panic, what was the protocol? Did one curtsey or salute first? We quickly got rid of uniform handbags, cameras, checked on stocking seams, our makeup, our hats on straight and lined up to attention, and there she was. I stepped forward and saluted smartly and a quick bob on shaking hands and prayed hard I would remember everyone's names and not have a mental block. I didn't, and all went well, she had recently returned from laying the very large and unusual foundation stone for our new depot and training establishment at the site of the Royal Pavilion, Aldershot, and spent at least ten minutes telling us all about it, how delighted she was and whom she had met; she said how pleased she had been to meet us all. I saluted and she was gone – we were all speechless! We retrieved our handbags and cameras and tucked in to our strawberries and cream. The three Canadians just couldn't believe what had happened, and Matron was a bit surprised too.

Coming back from lunch one day I found two soldiers in full uniform and boots and gaiters sitting outside my office door. Strange, I wasn't expecting anyone and boots and gaiters were not allowed for patients. They stood to attention as I approached and I saw one soldier had his rifle. The orderly handed me the notes and said he had been waiting for my return! Heading the notes in red ink was 'Soldier Under Sentence' taking me back to days at Colchester, as I hadn't seen an SUS since then.

On reading the notes I found the soldier had been found guilty of rape and grievous bodily harm at court martial in the north of Germany and had been sentenced to a stretch in the military prison at Shepton Mallet. I could hardly believe my eyes; he supposedly had a torn cartilage in the knee and persuaded some gullible doctor that it would be a good idea if he stopped off on the way to have it operated on, which in those days meant three weeks breakfast in bed and three weeks intensive physiotherapy to be fit to return to full duties.

I shot down that corridor like a bat out of hell, as the Canadians would say, to the colonel's office. Luckily he was in and I put the documents on his desk and said would he please get him discharged and on his way with his guard with the rifle as I was not going to have him on my ward. If his knee had locked in position and he had been on a stretcher it would have been a completely different matter, but if he had marched in, in boots and gaiters, he could certainly march out again. I think even the colonel was a bit shocked and proceeded to get him on his way en route for UK and prison.

Thank goodness for having served at Colchester, knowledge is a marvellous thing.

When on duty in the afternoon, at 1 pm the first job is to do a social round of the patients when the ward is quiet. We checked that all the patients were getting their mail sent on from their unit (soldiers' mail has a high priority in the army as it is good for morale). We checked that they had all the correct uniform necessary for discharge parade, and if we could help with any family problems in the UK. A sick soldier might need a birthday card or present for a family member and Dorothy, who was the welfare officer, would see to this for them. The Canadian soldiers had their own wardmaster who came to check their requirements.

Going into the eight-bedded ward the Canadian corporal in the first bed, who had been admitted the day before with a possible slipped disc, shot up on his hands and said, 'Have you come to give me a back rub, Sister?'

'No, but my orderly will be along at 2 pm with the back tray,' I said with a smile.

The next day a similar thing happened and this time, 'Now you know you would like to give me a back rub, Sister.'

'No, not tonight, Josephine.'

The next day he was really getting out of order. 'You know you would like to get your hands on my body, Sister' or words to that effect. The thought passed through my head that I would like to give him a back rub with something in my cupboard. There was complete silence in the ward and the boys were certainly not amused. On the other side of the ward was an 'old soldier', a sergeant from wartime.

'Any problems, Sergeant?'

'Only 'im over there, he's a right pain and we're fed up to the back teeth – can't you fix him, Sister?'

'Leave it to me.' How dare he upset my boys!

I went back to the office and sat at my desk with my head in my hands. If what I planned to do was to be successful then time was of the essence. I went to the sluice and picked up the back tray, my one orderly on duty was far away checking the laundry. I went to the medicine cupboard and reached for a dark green pharmacy bottle, heavily marked 'POISON – for external use only'. I checked the bottle and it hadn't been used for a long time. There had been some evaporation so it was going to be pretty strong; this was not an 'over-the-counter' from Boots the Chemist – this was British Army Pharmacy. I had to loosen the cork carefully, as it was stuck and that was the last thing I needed. I secured the cork and laid the bottle down on the tray. He was expecting a massage with warm soapy water, spirit to dry and harden the skin, and talcum powder to finish. I didn't want him to suspect anything different. I reckoned if this was going to be successful I needed a minimum of forty seconds and sixty seconds at the outside. I knew that a very large bath towel was on the locker, which I needed to protect the bed, as the fluid can stain.

I marched into the ward, grabbed one screen, threw it round the necessary part of the bed and said, 'Right, turn over on you left side and drop your pyjamas.' A vulgar expression I had never used before or since. Well! He really thought Christmas had come early. The boys were silent as they thought he had won. I carefully arranged the towel and draped the sheet discreetly round him. He was so busy poking his fingers through the screen and telling the boys he knew Sister wanted to get her hands all over him that he was unaware of anything different. I poured some of the thick fluid into my left palm and started to massage with the right palm. I started with the neck, shoulder blades, down the spine and he never flinched when I did the base of the back, I was just about to start on the back of the thighs and knees when several things happened. He stopped talking because he suddenly realised his shoulder blades were on fire and there was a rather pungent smell coming off him. The young soldier in the next bed caught a whiff and identified it and sent a stage whisper to the next bed. 'Sloane's Liniment' and the words flew round the ward and suddenly a football roar went up, so loud the orderly in the linen room decided he'd better investigate. I finished off the legs and feet, left the towel in place to protect the sheets, re-draped the sheet and was just putting the screen away as the door was thrust open.

'What's going on in here?' he said.

'Just Sister doing a back rub,' I replied and swept out with the tray. I didn't go back in the room again that day.

I was on late duty the next day and taking report from my junior sister at 1 pm. She remarked that the Canadian had asked the colonel if he could be discharged. 'Go out? You've only just come in,' said the colonel, but eventually was persuaded to release him on Saturday. Starting my usual round I found him flat on his back with a book close to his face. I politely asked him how he was twice, but had only a mumble for reply. I went to the next bed.

'Is he alright? He's not speaking to me.'

'He wasn't very happy last night at visiting time, Sister.'

'Oh, why? What happened?'

'His wife came and couldn't stand the smell so she sat and chatted to me all visiting time – it was lovely!' said the young soldier who rarely had visitors and he'd had a very pretty blonde at his bedside all evening.

I made my way round the ward, coming up to the old sergeant. 'Any problems, Sergeant?'

'None at all, Sister,' giving me a big wink. Reading between the lines I think the Canadian had been boasting of his prowess in bed, which hadn't gone down too well with a ward full of unaccompanied soldiers with wives, and girl friends back in UK as most were doing National Service. I don't think the Canadian would try it on again with a QA; he left on Saturday without saying goodbye. Sloane's Liniment could be found in most larders at home in the '40s and '50s alongside arrowroot, castor oil and arnica. It was an excellent pain reliever known as a counter irritant in the nursing profession along with the poultices we had to learn to apply. Wednesday afternoon was always used for sport in the army so all units would have a supply for treatment of sore knees, backs and shoulders, but perhaps Canadians were not familiar with it. I am told that now it can be used only for horses, not for humans!

Another patient in the Canadian Army who gave me a problem was in fact British. He had completed two years

National Service and asked to extend his time but was refused, which made me wonder what he had been up to. The lad then applied to the Canadian Army and had been accepted.

In 1960 the DH Lawrence book *Lady Chatterley's Lover* went to court on a charge of obscenity and was headline news. One night when eight of us were playing canasta a Scottish sister with the Canadians had remarked that the American PX (Post Exchange), the equivalent of our NAAFI (Navy, Army and Air Force Institutes), had been selling the unexpurgated copy in paperback for some time and she had a copy if anyone wanted to read it. I had remembered this bit of information when, months later, it became useful.

This patient was on three weeks bed rest after a knee operation and for three days had the book open on his bed table, which I had ignored. One day at 4 pm my QA nurse came into the office, obviously in some distress, saying could I deal with the patient as he had continually been making nasty suggestive remarks to her about the book. She was a nice girl and I knew she would not complain unduly. I told her not to go into that ward again and to tell me if anything else needed doing. I promised her I would deal with him but I needed to do some homework.

I went off at 5 pm for tea and caught the Scottish sister on the way to her room and asked if I could come and see her. I explained about the Canadian and said I hadn't time to read the book but could she suggest an incident in the book that makes a chap look a bit of a 'Charlie'. She thought hard and then said there was that part in the woods where they go off and pick wild flowers and then entwine them around parts of their anatomy, would that do? Perfectly, I noted chapter and page, as it was probably the identical copy. Armed with this knowledge I thanked her and left.

The next day Nurse wasn't on duty until 1 pm, which suited me fine, as I didn't want the patient to think she had come to me about him. I went into the ward to do my usual first round and the book was still open on the bed table at the bottom of the bed and I casually picked it up saying it was taking him a long time to read, he'd had it out for three days at least. 'DH Lawrence does make you men look a bit of a "Charlie" doesn't he? Especially that bit on page 69 where they pick wild flowers in the wood and ...' I didn't need to say any more, I looked up from the book and he had slid down the bed with the sheet over his mouth with both ears now like two red lamps against the white pillow and his face ashen – flushing can work in funny ways. I closed the book and moved on to finish my round and the boys all had bright laughing eyes – they hadn't been amused at his behaviour either.

When I had finished my report at 1 pm Nurse had already

done her round. 'Don't know what you said, Sister, but the book has disappeared and he won't speak to me.' 'Good,' I said and told her what I had done. This was another case when putting someone on a charge was not an option.

Another lasting memory from that ward comes to mind: one night a Polish soldier was brought in with a possible broken neck. He was a batman to one of the regimental colonels and when sleepwalking had fallen from a second-floor window in barracks. He had a terrible history, his father had been killed by the Germans and his mother raped and murdered by the Russians and he was still subject to nightmares, although a competent batman.

He was nursed flat with a neck support but we were worried that if he felt sick with the head injury he might do more damage to the neck. I had the task of passing a fine Rhyles tube up his nose and down into his stomach so that the contents could be aspirated. I have never seen such terror as in his eyes when I approached the bed with the tray. I put the tray down and knelt on the floor beside him and taking his hand in mine tried to explain why it was so important to do this and would he let me? It didn't matter how long it took but I would help him all the way. It took a long time gently coaxing him every inch of the way but we did it and I told him well done. Fortunately it didn't stay down for long; we found nothing too seriously wrong and he was allowed up with a support collar. He seemed to follow me around doing any jobs which needed to be done and I would often find a small jar with a rose or other flower on my desk in the morning. He did go back to his unit after a few weeks with us but I hope I never have to witness such terror in anyone's eyes again.

Shortly after I arrived in Iserlohn there was an advert on the notice board for an old 1950 Opel car for sale at DM 800 (about £55). I hadn't driven a car since Ghana but I would need one here. I asked a friend to check it over and there didn't seem to be any problems so I bought it. It was a great old car in battleship grey with a rather long bonnet – one friend with a mini used to ask me if the bonnet could go round corners! It had bench seats back and front, the gear stick was on the steering wheel, a very efficient heater, a radio and a crash gearbox so I had to learn how to double declutch each time I changed gear and it kept me on the road for three and a half years.

There was only one blip on its record – driving alone down the autobahn to Wuppertal to have lunch with friends, I suddenly had a smell of petrol and my 'full' petrol gauge was moving rapidly in front of my eyes. My one fear was that there might be an explosion and fire, but I put my foot down hoping for the next petrol station and garage to appear on the right hand side. As the finger moved through 'empty' I drove into a petrol station. A young man came out immediately from the garage. In halting German and sign language I explained what had happened. He lifted the bonnet, looked and disappeared back into the garage. He reappeared with a tin in his hand full of nuts, bolts, washers and many other small items one finds in garages. He picked out something like a metal-capped nut and screwed it onto the carburettor, started the car, checked that all was well and closed the bonnet saying ,'No charge, Fräulein.' I filled up with petrol, gave him a good tip and was safely on my way for lunch. That was service for you. I always found the young Germans were particularly kind and one would always offer to help with luggage at railway stations whether we were in uniform or not.

We did well for Bank Holidays as we had British, German and Canadian ones. I had some excellent National Service boys as RAMC orderlies; they didn't want to be there but they made the best of it. I found them efficient and kind and compassionate to their patients. One day coming back on duty I found three boys chatting in the corridor, one was on nights off and the other two had the weekend off. I asked them what they were going to do with their time off. They replied 'nothing much', as they really couldn't afford to go very far. I thought this was an awful waste of time when they could have seen such interesting parts of Germany. On impulse I asked them if they would like to borrow my old car and go down the Rhine and see something of the country. My gut instinct told me they would look after it but at £55 it wasn't the end of the world if they wrote it off and it was only insured third party, fire and theft. Military personnel owning cars had a monthly ration of petrol very cheaply; we paid through the unit and received petrol coupons that could be exchanged at most large garages. I had plenty so there would be no cost to the boys apart from food and a bed for the nights they were away. Their faces lit up and with thanks they accepted my keys and coupons.

They had a lovely few days and told me all about the places they had visited on their return. One of them was a locomotive engineer, but all seemed interested in engines and cars. On days off they would frequently go round scrap yards seeing what they could find and over the months I was asked if I would like a nearly new rear seat which I could get for a few DM and they would fit it for me and several other parts for the car. Before they left at the end of their two years they asked if I would like a newer engine fitted which they had found and I agreed. They did the work over the weekend in the motor transport workshops in the hospital grounds using the equipment and hoists, etc. They must have had friends in high places because it was out of bounds to me!

The only time they actually asked to borrow the car was to visit the Nürburgring for a motor racing day before they left Germany and I think it was a rather special day for them. One of them decided to stay in the RAMC and before I left had two stripes on his arm, had almost finished his nurse training and had married a QA nurse. The other two returned to their trades in the UK and I hope they felt that National Service hadn't been too bad after all.

Many of the Canadian regiments were based around Hemer where there was a Canadian Army school. The music teacher was very involved with the Hemer Amateur Musical Society and each year she put on an excellent Gilbert and Sullivan Operetta. In '63 they put on 'The Mikado', a boy friend had been in 'Pirates' the year before and said what fun it was and persuaded me to join.

I was a little apprehensive as I hadn't been in a choir since a teenager in the Sheffield Children's Choir when we put on a performance in the City Hall once a year.

We rehearsed for over three months and it took me almost the first month before I could reach all the high notes in the finale to Act I but I got there in the end. It was completely international – British, Canadian, French Canadian, Dutch and German – and it was amazing to me how all the different accents disappeared in singing voices. We gave six performances to packed audiences in the Club

Soldatenheim at Hemer and it was a wonderful experience I wouldn't have missed for anything.

Sometimes on Sunday afternoons we would drive to the Mohner Dam, the scene of the first target of the Dambusters. One could sit and have tea or coffee close by and the rebuilt large breach in the dam could be clearly seen. To me it was identical to the Ladybower and Derwent Dams complete with the twin towers and wooded hillsides where the bombers did their practice runs in preparation, frightening the sheep and the farmers complaining to the local paper about the number of ewes miscarrying. It was the only place in the world where I could feel homesick for Derbyshire and I enjoyed those quiet moments there.

In the autumn of '63 I was coming to the end of my three-and-a-half-year tour of Germany. I had been held back to sort out a gynaecological problem, which had defeated two consultants, but in '62 a new consultant arrived who in the future would be appointed the Director General of Army Medical Services. He solved the problem and as a result of his care I was able to produce a healthy son in 1972 for whom these memories are being recorded.

I was now fit for service anywhere in the world and had done my senior officer's course at the Depot and passed my exams for promotion from captain to major which would take place in London Millbank Military Hospital in 1966.

Matron sent for me one day and asked where I would like to be posted to now. 'Singapore please, Ma'am,' I replied.

In October 1963 I left Germany with a light heart for two weeks embarkation leave at home in Sheffield and the anticipation of adventures to come in the Far East.

In July 1954, following the state finals, I was finally able to wear the long cap, the hallmark of an SRN.

My father, Warrant Officer II George Madin MM, served in the First World War in the Royal Field Artillery.

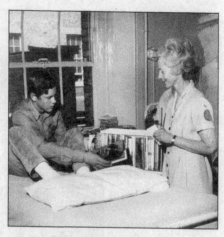

Dorothy a British Red Cross and
St. John's welfare officer, who worked
with me in Colchester and Germany,
doing the book rounds.

Opening of the new QA officers' mess in Colchester with Lt. Col.
Dowling and DGMS, 1956. [Courtesy of *The Nursing Mirror*]

The geckos in Ghana were silent until one made a disparaging remark about someone in the mess when a mixture between a chuckle and a tut tut seemed to emerge from them.

The 'thing' seemed to be sitting on its haunches and boxing with its front legs. I moved fast, grabbed a towel and shot up the verandah calling to the sister: 'There's something nasty in the bathroom.'

General Paley (left) with President Kwame Nkrumah (centre) and George (second from right), who taught me to drive in Ghana.

As we approached Bolgatanga market on foot we could hear
the cacophony of sound issuing forth from the 'mammies',
who ran the entire market.

On one trip to northern Ghana I visited Kumasi, Tamele
and Bolgatanga, which was almost on the border of French
Togoland, and stayed in a hut like this.

Margaret McDermott and self in Germany.

'Doing Europe' with Canadian sisters in Germany.
Heidelberg, on the river Neckar, appeared suspended
in a medieval time warp with its 14th century castle,
medieval alleyways and old bridge.

Dorothy, the welfare officer from Colchester,
was posted to Germany and we took a
boat up the Danube to Vienna, visiting the
Schönbrunn Palace.

BMH Iserlohn was one of several BAOR (British Army
of the Rhine) military hospitals in Germany
and was housed in a converted Panzer barracks.

En route to Singapore I stopped at Gan Island in the
Indian Ocean, an RAF staging post in the Addu Atoll
and part of the Maldives.

I travelled to Singapore aboard a Comet jet aircraft of the Queen's
Flight with Sir Edmund and Lady Huddleston. On arrival in Gan
Island, Lady Huddleston said to the stewards, 'Get the girls' luggage
off, they may like a swim,' which we blessed her for as we were still in
the clothes we had left in on Sunday and it was now Tuesday.

The big white veil of the QAs was
a morale boost for wounded troops
evacuated to Singapore from the
Confrontation in Borneo.

Tins of Milo on the tray,
which kept us going through
the night in the operating
theatre in Singapore.

British Military Hospital, Alexandra Road, Singapore, was one of
the biggest hospitals in Southeast Asia, four times the size of the wing
shown below. A bicycle would have been useful on night duty!

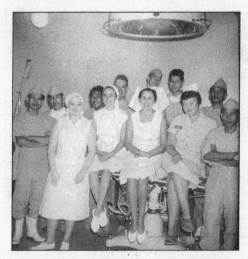

I am seated centre and surrounded by theatre
staff in British Military Hospital, Singapore.

On Christmas Day 1963, patients at BMH Singapore were
visited by an admiral instead of a lord mayor as would have
been the case in the UK.

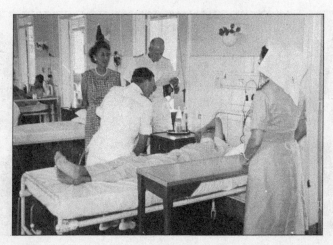

Peggy Grey, me, Mary Higginbotham and Janet
Gillies at a sister's wedding in the QA mess in
BMH Singapore.

Post-party breakfast at 1am in the wardroom of HMS *London* with
Cdr Mike Howard-Smith (left) and Cdr Ken Wilcoxson (right).

On holiday in Hong Kong, 1965, with Irene Cathcart, who snaps the CO in an embarrassing position.

Seeing Macau on a shoestring with my pedicab driver, who took me round the island.

Golden Sand Hotel in Penang, Malaysia, was a favourite of ours for much-needed R&R (rest and recuperation).

In full QA uniform outside the military
hospital in Millbank, London, 1966.

On duty for Her Majesty at the Queen's birthday
parade of Trooping the Colour, 1967.

Under my watchful eye, two civilian nurses view the
Florence Nightingale communion set at the Military Silver
Exhibition held in the Town Hall in Chester, 1970. I am
joined by retired nursing officer Major Pegg.

Getting back on my feet at Osborne House
Convalescent Home for Officers on the Isle of White
following a nasty infection.

Lyn (WRAF), Sue (WRAC) and me (QARANC),
all Women's Services Liaison Officers, on a visit
to RN Air Station Brawdy in Wales.

Me, Sheila, Sue and Lyn on a liaison visit to find
information about the WRNS.

Clare with baby Ian, Dom and Alan at Ruthin Castle.

Margaret McDermott, Clare and Dom at Ian's christening, 14 May 1972.

Alan and Ian at the Italianate-style village of Portmeirion in Wales, 1975.

IN AND AROUND RUTHIN

Ruthin woman's Red Cross honour from the Queen

ACCOMPANIED by her husband and her mother, a Ruthin woman recently attended at Buckingham Palace to receive from the Queen her award as an Associate Member of the Royal Red Cross.

Mrs Margaret Thomas, of 7 Erw Goch, Ruthin, was formerly a major in Queen Alexandra's Royal Army Nursing Corps. She was in the service for 16 years, the latter four years as liaison officer for HQ Western Command. This involved lecturing on Army careers to girls at schools and colleges in the whole of Wales and part of the North-West. She retired from the service last year.

Mrs Thomas was born in Sheffield and her husband comes from Manchester. Mr Thomas is employed by the Wales Gas Board, and they have lived in Ruthin for the past three years. They have a son, Ian James, aged eight months.

Pictured outside Buckingham Palace with Major Margaret Thomas are her husband, Alan, and her mother, Mrs Blanche Madin, of Sheffield, who celebrated her 80th birthday this year.

The local paper in Ruthin, north Wales, reports on the investiture at Buckingham Palace, 30 November 1972. I am flanked by Alan and my mother.

8

Singapore

October 1963 – October 1965

British Military Hospital Singapore was one of the busiest hospitals in Southeast Asia, close to Borneo and involved in the Indonesian Confrontation, as the campaign was known.

In 1962 President Sukarno of Indonesia sought to prevent the absorption of the former British colonies in Borneo into Malaysia at Independence. There was an extended campaign of subversion and infiltration by his regular army into Sabah, Sarawak and the very pro-British small sultanate of Brunei, which now all belonged to Malaysia.

The Gurkhas, commandos and supporting units were all operating there and The Royal Navy, The Royal Fleet Auxiliary (RFA supply ships) and a fleet of aircraft carriers (making more than fifty ships over the four years) gave support to the newly formed Federation of Malaysia.

The RAF, also giving support, had their own hospital at Changi but were involved in all our casualty evacuations.

All naval cold cases and casualties came to BMH Singapore, also known as Alexandra Hospital, which was the base hospital for the campaigns. We also looked after all service families and Public Works Department personnel who gave support to the services.

I had no idea that the journey out to the Far East would be such an adventure. I had expected a flight of at least twenty-four hours, with a couple of stops for refuelling, in a Britannia turbo prop aircraft full of service personnel.

Shortly before I was due to leave the house, a phone call from the MOD said I was to ignore my movement order and to await further instructions. Several days later they arrived and saying farewell to my elderly parents I set off for Swindon on the first leg of the journey. Changing trains at Swindon I was called to the station master's office over the tannoy and told to return to Sheffield, with no further explanation.

Saying goodbye for two years to parents in their seventies is never easy as they are thinking they may never see you again. I decided to telephone the QA Depot at Hindhead and speak to an old friend to see if there was a possibility of staying there until called again. She rang back to say a major who was proceeding on leave had offered me her room for as long as I needed it, an excellent idea while awaiting further orders. I said goodbye once more and proceeded to the depot. My orders then came to report to RAF Lyneham on the Sunday afternoon.

On arrival things did not seem as expected. There were very few people about other than a QA Lieutenant Thomas, who had been on my movement order, and ten smartly turned-out naval officers in mufti. Clare, the QA, and I introduced ourselves and it was obvious that she was in my age group of thirty plus, which was nice for company on the journey; six years later she would become my sister-in-law. After a meal we returned early to our accommodation as we had been warned we would be called in the early hours ready for embarkation. Going through emigration the RAF corporal asked me if I had an overnight bag with me and to keep it by me. We were then escorted out to a gleaming silver aircraft sitting on the tarmac.

After we had taken off it was explained that we were on a Comet jet aircraft of the Queen's Flight taking Sir Edmund and Lady Huddleston and retinue on an inspection flight of transport command and for security reasons we would not be told the next place of call until we were airborne each time. We were settled down with blankets and lights were dimmed, having been told we would be called in time to prepare for disembarkation at El Adem, a staging post in north Africa not far from Tobruk, and in time for breakfast. Descending in the plane the station looked the size of a postage stamp in the desert with sand as far as the eye could see and we wondered if we would make it down safely, it looked so tiny. We did of course and to this day I remember the wonderful piping hot fry up for breakfast and we all tucked in as though we hadn't eaten for a week. All too soon we were embarking on this beautiful aircraft again and the next stop was Nairobi, where we would say goodbye to the naval officers who were to join their ship at Mombasa.

We arrived in Nairobi mid-afternoon and travelled down a beautiful boulevard lined with bougainvillea in varieties of reds, purples and white; even in Ghana I had never seen such colours. We were taken to our hotel in central Nairobi and after a meal were able to have a quick look round outside before an early night. After breakfast we were once again off on our travels, this time across the Indian Ocean to a small RAF staging post called Gan, situated at the bottom of a group of islands in a coral atoll known as the Maldives, completely unknown to us at the time.

Before lunch we were invited to pre-lunch drinks with the VIPs in the Queen's Lounge at the rear of the aircraft (the naval officers had been invited the day before). It was a most comfortable area with blue carpet and all the seating in a shade of blue with uncut moquette upholstery and hidden behind curtains two bunks for sleeping facilities, most interesting to see. Clare, being a midwife from Germany, had much to chat about with Lady Huddleston, as they had just had a grandchild born in a British military hospital on BAOR (British Army of the Rhine). We had a very pleasant hour before returning to the cabin for lunch. After lunch we both had a sleep and on waking got our things organised for the next stop. Two different stewards passing our seats stopped by and quietly advised 'Lock your doors and windows tonight, Sisters' and moved on. This rather amused us and when the second steward confidentially told us the same thing we demanded to know what all this was about. He told us we were landing on a very small island, the runway was only one mile long and the width of the island, and so if the reverse thrust to brake wasn't correct we could get our feet wet. It had 650 RAF personnel working there unaccompanied for nine months and females were taboo. Only one WRVS lady was allowed, who had to be be thirty-five years old at least! The RAF boasted it could refurbish an aircraft and send it on its way faster than anywhere in the world and handled 7000 transit passengers monthly, refuelling their aircraft and providing food and relaxation in the hutted Blue Lagoon Hotel. This visit was going to be quite an experience and we understood the warnings. Clare remarked, 'We should be so lucky!'

We had always been asked to leave the plane by the

rear exit leaving the VIPs and retinue to descend to the red carpet. We gathered our belonging together and heard Lady Huddleston say to the stewards, 'Get the girls' luggage off, they may like a swim,' which we blessed her for as we were still in the clothes we had left in on Sunday and it was now Tuesday. We were in the tropics and the rig of the day should be cotton dresses and sandals. We hadn't once glanced out of the windows but proceeded together to the exit when asked to. We stood at the top of the steps and there below us, come to view the sisters on board were what looked like 650 boys, stripped to the waist, arms akimbo, as brown as the local Maldivians in several ranks of a very large semicircle.

The hot air of the tropics was rising and I could feel my skirt beginning to lift. My one thought was of Marilyn Monroe standing over a hot air grate and her circular skirt rising to waist high. I said, 'For goodness sake, Clare, hold your skirt down or there will be a riot down there.' We descended as sedately as possible with our hands full and with a big smile to the boys went across the red carpet. We were taken to our quarters in the middle of several long rows of single-storied accommodation blocks – twin bedded room with our own bathroom and overhead fans as usual for the tropics. Thanks to Lady Huddleston we were able to unpack, bath and change all our clothes for cottons. We managed to get in a quick look at the island but there was no time for a swim in the crystal clear water. I photographed a very interesting signpost showing the direction and mileage of fifteen RAF destinations including London (5750 miles), Nairobi (2510 miles) and Singapore (2135 miles) from this very beautiful tropical staging post. We joined the officers in the mess for dinner and drinks and a chat in the bar afterwards, returning to our quarters well before 10 pm.

By 11 pm we were in bed with the lights off and quietly chatting about the flight and how lucky we were to have two nights in a proper bed. Suddenly we heard a set of footsteps approaching on the wooden verandah, surprising because we didn't think any one else was lodging in our row. The footsteps came closer, stopped and someone struggled to get a key in the door.

'Someone's trying to get in,' whispered Clare.

They were still struggling so I said in a clear voice, 'I think you have got the wrong door.' There was a slight pause and then 'terribly sorry' and footsteps moved away. We were almost hysterical with laughter.

Next morning, at breakfast in the mess, we were eyeing the men at the table wondering which one it was, as we were sure it was an officer and suddenly one of the crew leaned across and said he thought he owed us an apology as he had obviously got the wrong room last night. I said, 'Please don't apologise, you made our day. If someone hadn't tried to get in after all the warnings we would have been very disappointed!' After breakfast our luggage was collected and we embarked for the last time on the final leg of our journey to Singapore.

On our arrival at RAF Changi we said our thanks to all on board and then proceeded through airport checks. I was surprised to find no QA sister or transport to meet us, as on arrival even at 4 am in the morning, there was always someone to meet the plane. We therefore got a taxi to BMH Singapore sisters' mess. In the mess we met a rather unhappy deputy matron; she had been expecting us on the previous Monday and had no idea where we had been, so we had to explain. The deputy is always responsible for the duty rosters so Clare was supposed to be on duty the day we arrived. The rules said we must have two days stand down to get over the jet lag, so that didn't please her. Two days later Clare went on duty on maternity and I didn't see much of her again. I proceeded by train to Kuala Lumpur to do two weeks relief theatre at BMH Kinrara, where I had a very gentle breaking in with theatre only working in the mornings.

During the Borneo Emergency work went on at top pressure in Singapore. In the acute surgical and resuscitation ward of sixty beds the very seriously ill patients were queuing up to get in the air-conditioned unit of ten beds. This unit was very necessary to be able to calculate fluid balance accurately in the high humidity of Singapore. It was not unusual to have three patients on respirators at one time and not always possible to have them nursed together, this presented a staffing problem as Matron had to provide a round the clock team for each one. In the case of an electrical breakdown a team from the patients unit was always on standby to come in and work the respirator by hand to keep the patient alive, luckily this never happened in my two years.

In the two main theatres (the third one was fracture theatre on another floor) we would be doing twenty to thirty routine cases a day and if one was 'on call' one would start again late evening when the RAF flew in cases of gunshot wounds to Changi. At first all these men would have been plucked out of the jungle by helicopters when our security forces had made sure it was safe to do so. Sometimes they would have been waiting for rescue for over twenty-four hours, but they were certainly tough – if they survived the journey and reached us then they all survived, which was quite remarkable. The few deaths I remember were road traffic accidents.

All patients with gunshot wounds were bed bathed

on admission and the filthy, stinking field dressings and uniforms were removed, along with leeches and creepy crawlies, as they had been in the jungle possibly for days. They were then prepared for the theatre. The theatre sister and team on call would aim to have a hot meal and bath and we could change out of uniform and into a dress and sandals before return to the hospital to prepare for the boys.

The aim was then to complete a 'débridement' of all wounds, which was the opening of wounds and removal of all dead and very damaged tissue and any foreign bodies such as bullets and debris associated with them. The channels were then syringed with a solution of hydrogen peroxide, as the bug causing gas gangrene is anaerobic and can't survive in oxygen. The wounds were left open, unstitched, with dressings for five to six days, draining and starting the healing process. In the wards we used a lot of EUSOL (Edinburgh University Solution of Lime) dressings for cleaning up dirty wounds, which was a fantastic lotion, gentle to the patient and didn't sting – I'm not sure if it is used now. In five or six days, when they were ready, we had them back in theatre for suturing the wound and often skin grafts to the exit wounds, which presented much skin loss.

Dealing with the patients took all night and we were lucky if we finished between 5 am and 6 am. At about 4 am I would line up mugs of Milo, the Nestlé chocolate drink full of calories, vitamins and salts, which kept us all going that little bit longer. They all laughed, calling me 'Milo Madin' but they drank it and it worked! When the last patient left it was all hands on deck to scrub out the theatre and start preparing for the next shift on at 8 am. All the drums had to be repacked with clean green towels, sheets and gowns ready for resterilizing in the autoclaves. All instruments had to be washed and crated ready for sterilizing and supplies renewed. It was then away for our breakfast and sleep until teatime – a good twenty-four hours work well done. All theatre sisters and staff worked at this pressure for many months, maybe years, but it was very rewarding.

Later in the year we had a military ward opened in Brunei and Kuching staffed in each place by two sisters and a full team of RAMC personnel giving primary care and rest to casualties before evacuation to Singapore. Clare was the first midwife to be allowed to go for a three-month tour in Brunei and after missing her RAF flight cadged a lift on the Sultan's private plane at his invitation. What the sergeant in Brunei said when he heard a midwife was being posted in I understand is unrepeatable! This improvement in care for the casualties certainly helped to improve the theatre sisters' sleep patterns – we still had night emergencies but we at least got back to bed. Clare said when the stretchers were being unloaded she could hear some of the boys say, 'You'll

be alright now, mate, the QAs are here. I can see them.'
Again that big white veil adding to the morale of the troops.

One day I was reading the new patients' notes and the
very distinctive neat handwriting seemed familiar. I turned
the page to see the signature and yes, there was a very
familiar name from Colchester seven years before. A young
RAMC officer who had grumbled and complained about
the army throughout his National Service found he couldn't
settle in civvy street after two years with us. He was now a
regular captain doing good work in the jungles of Borneo –
last known to have retired as a full colonel!

My two years rotated between acute surgical and
orthopaedic wards, theatre, night superintendent and every
four months two weeks leave known as R&R (rest and
recuperation). All personnel had to fly out of Singapore for
nights off or leave so that there was no chance of being
recalled for duty. Two sisters out of the night teams always
finished together so there was always someone to go away
with. Peggy, an Australian girl, and I became good friends
and often had our leave together. Her parents had emigrated
from Leeds to Australia in the 1930s and she had lived and
nurse trained in Perth and then joined the QAs. She was
good company and we both had the same sense of humour.
For nights off we usually flew to Penang and booked into the
comfortable Golden Sands Hotel at Batu Ferringhi. It was

then a single-storied building but right on the beach, twin rooms with air-conditioning and en-suite bath; it was bliss. With many tables outside under the palm trees we could have all our meals outside if we so wished, they were all lit by lamps at night. The Golden Sands is now something of a skyscraper in appearance, I'm told. By 8.30 pm we were ready for bed and slept round the clock – at least twelve hours – to breakfast under the palms about 9.30 am. We read, dozed, swam and after lunch back to bed by 2 pm, two hours sleep, delicious tea, sandwiches, huge slices of paw paw with lime and sugar, perhaps a walk on the beach before dinner. By 8.30 pm we couldn't keep our eyes open any longer and back to bed; we kept this routine up for over seven days. One evening, waiting for dinner, we saw a crowd of girls all laughing together come into the grounds – we watched them for a time and then looked at each other and said 'nurses'. They were New Zealand military nurses from the hospital at Butterworth on the mainland and had come over by ferry for an evening meal at the hotel. We introduced ourselves and joined them after dinner for a walk on the moonlit beach. Suddenly they started to sing their Maori songs and it was quite magical as it travelled far in the still night. The hotel guests fell silent and listened, spellbound. An experience I shall never forget. We were quite sad to say goodbye.

On the last full day we decided we must make an effort and took a taxi into the capital, Georgetown, and shopped. We had morning coffee in the famous Eastern & Oriental Hotel, very reminiscent of colonial times. After lunch we took the cable car 2500 feet up above sea level to Penang Hill Hotel where they served afternoon tea in an English cottage garden with all manner of English plants and flowers. The only unusual one was a creeper very much like a version of wisteria climbing over a pergola but the flower racemes were very large and a vivid jade green like a bunch of large grapes. All too soon it was time to return to the hotel and pack, tomorrow we would fly back refreshed and ready for anything once more. This routine was carried out for the first week of any R&R, by the second week we were fit enough to do some sightseeing.

In September 1964 I made my first visit to Hong Kong alone for two weeks R&R as no one else was free to go. It had been a particularly heavy month previously and many had been going without proper off duty. The commanding officer and matron agreed it was imperative for R&R to continue otherwise there could be health problems. I couldn't book into BMH Bowen Road Hong Kong Island as they were very full so I stayed in a good Chinese hotel about two miles up Nathan Road on the mainland. It was ideal for R&R, fourteen floors to it, quiet, air-conditioned with private bath and at the touch of a bell a boy would appear with tea and toast and the morning paper and one could sleep as long as one wished.

The RAF had given me a free 'indulgence' flight and apologised for asking for £1-6s-8d for my meals on board. We had flown into Saigon, South Vietnam, for refuelling and it was like Little America. Coming down in the plane, we were forbidden to use any cameras but there were hundreds of helicopters as far as the eye could see. I managed to send off two envelopes already stamped like first day covers to my nephews to prove I'd been there. On taking off again we were told we were travelling in the possible path of Typhoon Sally, expected to reach Hong Kong that evening.

There was a very British atmosphere in Hong Kong which seemed quite different to Singapore, the people appeared so placid going about their business not knowing if they would have a home by midnight. We had seen thousands of little boats tied up in typhoon shelters, we understood that blood donor sessions were going on all day and the most vulnerable people were evacuated with their few possessions to schools and welfare centres so they had a roof over their head for the night.

Buildings like our hotel had the glass doors boarded up and criss-cross masking tape was applied to smaller windows, just like wartime Britain, to prevent them shattering and injuring people. As evening approached storm signals were hoisted to 8 and only taxis and emergency vehicles were allowed on the roads and we were locked in. That evening as I couldn't leave the hotel I made my way to the bar for a long drink and took a book to read. Looking round there appeared to be only one European in the bar, a man standing at the bar in a possible uniform of white shirt and black tie. I said a courteous good evening and he turned out to be a BOAC flight engineer and came from Blackpool! Considering we were more than 8,000 miles away from home he seemed to be a neighbour. He was leaving on an early morning flight but said he would be back on Friday and would look out for me. I must have looked pretty haggard at the time as on the Friday I was on the way out of the hotel and he passed me with barely a glance, did a double-take when he arrived at the lift, looked back and said, 'Good Lord, woman, you look better!' We agreed to have a meal together that evening and afterwards went to the Crows Nest at the top of the Hilton Hotel, sat at the bar and listened to Matt Monroe in person entertaining the diners for free – my favourite singer of the time. I remember walking back up Nathan Road with shoes in my hands and the pavement being still warm from the heat of the day. About every three to four months he would turn up in Singapore early morning, phone at 6.30 am to say he'd just landed and was off to bed and could he take me to Raffles for dinner. A lovely evening and always someone happy to do my 'on call'.

The second week I was able to meet Anne, an old friend from Iserlohn and now at Bowen Road. She took me round the island and we had afternoon tea colonial style at Repulse Bay Hotel. The shops were like lots of Bond Street all rolled into one and I visited Lane & Crawford's to purchase my first real pearls. I couldn't afford a suitable posh clasp – that would come the next year. We always had to carry our return fare in case the RAF couldn't help and this time I travelled with the lovely Cathay Pacific airline and I still have the beautiful menu card as a memento, travelling in style I returned fully refreshed from a lovely holiday.

The Prime Minister, Tunku Abdul Rahman, insisted that all British servicemen taking part in the campaign were known as 'security forces' and therefore casualties were hidden in overall numbers so the British public at home were kept very much in the dark about what was really going on in Malaysia.

Army public relations staff would often follow up the badly injured patients in BMH for reports for local papers back in their home towns. When looking through some old papers I came across an old newspaper cutting of a badly injured Royal Marine commando in my ward and the first draft of a case history of a bad burns I was asked to do for Colonel Gordon, our matron (later to become brigadier and matron-in-chief), which was to be forwarded to MOD.

The marine had been caught in an Indonesian ambush at a house in the jungle and several of the patrol were killed. He was plucked out of the jungle by helicopter with bullet wounds to both lungs, left foot and right leg. These were the dangers our boys faced every day with little acknowledgement by Malaysia at the time. He was eighteen years old and the bravest lad, never complaining after many operations and soon to be a 'casevac' (casualty evacuation) with the RAF, who would have to fly relatively low all the way to UK to keep the pressure even in the lungs.

It was rare to have a 'moaner' but I had a sapper in from Thailand where the Royal Engineers were helping to build an airstrip and roads. He had a routine nose operation to help with his breathing. When Matron's inspection was over in the mornings the up-patients were free to visit the Red Cross department on request, where they could relax and play table tennis, cards, board games, do handicrafts, listen to music but nothing seemed to suit this lad from the food to the games. When he was discharged he came to say goodbye, saying 'I expect you will be glad to see the back of me, Sister, but remember bad pennies often turn up again!' I laughed and told him to get along.

Many weeks later when I had done a spell of night duty and then taken over the surgical and resuscitation ward of sixty beds, we had a signal to say a patient was coming in from Thailand, via RAF Changi with a QA escort, with severe and extensive flame burns. A petrol stove had exploded spraying him with burning petrol and he was only wearing shorts, socks and boots at the time. He had second- and third-degree burns of the chest, abdomen and back, the entire right arm including the palm and the ulna border of the left arm, and both legs from high thigh to boot tops. At least half was anaesthetic, that is, painless, as the nerves had been damaged.

He was being transferred from an American hospital in Thailand where he had been held for forty-eight hours for primary care and listed seriously ill. He travelled on a stryker frame, which I was familiar with and had used once before. This was a mobile metal stretcher frame on wheels, which enabled the patient to be turned from his back to his front with the minimum of handling. He would be sandwiched between another identical stretcher, clamped together with wing nuts either end and swiftly revolved with a handle and then the original stretcher quickly removed. Ideal for the treatment of burns as it relieves pressure at regular intervals.

On arrival at the ward two intravenous drips were running, his face was as black as the rest of him and completely unrecognisable. As the stryker approached me a voice loud and clear said, 'Hi,Sister, I told you bad pennies always turn up again'. I just couldn't believe it was our moaner back!

The American hospital had done an excellent job and started him on a strict regime, which we continued. He was nursed in the first space in the ten-bed air-conditioned unit, which was essential as there is a terrible loss of fluid with burns – they weep incessantly and it is essential to get the fluid balance accurate. We used complete aseptic techniques as though we were in the operating theatre to avoid any infection of the open areas. Within forty-eight hours we had him on a normal bed between sterile sheets, covering the pillows and every thing else. The four-hourly routine in daytime was to gently clean all burns with Phisohex (an anti-bacterial scrub used in theatre) removing any dead skin from the blisters with sterile forceps and scissors then spraying with penicillin powder and leaving burns exposed to dry. He would be walked around the bed once a day to keep the limbs moving to prevent scar tissue contracting, it was quite exhausting for him but when he understood the reason he agreed to co-operate.

His mum arrived from UK and she was a marvellous support to him and us! It took anything from forty minutes to do the dressings and then we would be back again in four hours. We shut our ears to the abuse he showered on us as he saw us approaching with the trolley and mum would be heard to say, 'Don't you talk to the sisters like that' from the other side of the screen! He demanded steak and chips every day and had it for about six weeks. We gave him painkillers half an hour before doing the dressings and heavily sedated him at night to give him the strength to cope with the day. As the areas became dry we left them alone so the crust hopefully would separate.

At seventeen days after admission we were allowed to start saline baths to cleanse all the areas thoroughly and to get the limbs moving with gentle exercises in the water. With the help of two strong orderlies we put him into a large Victorian bath filled with warm saline, and two sisters knelt on thick towels on the terrazzo floor either side of the bath, and gently sponged all areas, moving the limbs. After a few minutes there was a yell from him and he cried, 'I'm pink! I'm pink!' When we looked there was quite a dramatic floating away of the black crusts on the top of the water. We looked at each other across the bath and we all had tears rolling down our cheeks. All our hard work and battles with him had paid off and he was well on the way to recovery.

The inner thighs which had taken the full blast and were deep third degree were beginning to be ready for skin grafting if we could find a bit of normal skin to graft – we had to use postage stamp sizes eventually. He proceeded to make an uneventful recovery with good movement in all his limbs and we sent him up to the cool Cameron Highlands to convalesce. When seen at outpatients he seemed to have made a complete recovery and returned to Thailand.

We worked hard and every three months for a short time we played hard too, in the nicest possible way. During my two years in Singapore the aircraft carriers HMS *Hermes*, *Centaur*, *Victorious* and *Bulwark* all called in at various times when on tour of the Far East. We went on board each one for cocktail parties. These were held on the enormous lift, which normally brought up the aircraft, with folded wings, from the hold to the flight deck. The lift was stopped somewhere half way and we would descend by a gangway to the party. Before leaving, the Royal Marine Band would play on deck for the Ceremony of Evening Colours with the lowering of the White Ensign and Union Jack at 9 pm, known to us as the tune 'Sunset' – a very moving service at sea which brought many a tear to the eye.

Our social life was either a feast or a famine. With aircraft carriers also came two RFA supply ships flying the Blue Ensign and for many months the missile destroyer HMS *London*. For a few of us this became our favourite ship, possibly because it was smaller and we were able to get to know many of the officers on board. I would sometimes be dining alone having come off duty rather late after a long day and a colleague would come into the dining room dressed for a party and say 'when you have finished supper, Margaret, go and bathe and change and we'll wait for you, there's a spare seat in the car and we are going to "London" for a party.' They didn't ask if I would like to go; it was rather like a royal command. One did as one was told and exchanged uniform for a dress and high heels and drove fifteen miles to the naval base HMS *Terror*.

Walking up the gangway I would be asking myself: what am I doing here when I could be in my bed? At the top of the gangway the duty officer of the day would salute you and maybe the captain was also there waiting to shake hands and thank you for coming to join his officers and say how much it was appreciated as they had been at sea for three months. You arrived in the wardroom, were given a drink and met by thirty or more handsome officers in 'Red Sea rig' – red cummerbund, white shirt – eager to chat, dance and generally entertain. They were marvellous parties; the majority were quite senior officers probably because of the speciality of the ship, extremely entertaining and very good fun with the usual inter-service banter. About midnight breakfast would be served, bacon and eggs and beautiful hot crisp bread rolls straight from the galley ovens, we were escorted off the base just before 1 am, back in bed by 2 am and early morning call at 6.30 am, but one felt so much better for the change of scenery. It was a tonic. We kept to a code of behaviour as we assumed everyone was married unless proved otherwise and we advised all the young sisters the same, to try and avoid any broken hearts. We also had our own mess parties to return hospitality at this time.

On the Saturdays they were in port, a group of officers would come to collect several sisters at the mess and take us to a rather small, select nightclub, The Cockpit, in Singapore. We had a lovely meal and danced the night away to many of Matt Monro's songs, who was touring at the time. They were off again on exercises all too soon and our break was over.

The orthopaedic ward included a good mix of routine cases and casualties transferred from next door in resuscitation when out of danger. Some patients always stayed in the memory for various reasons.

The insurgents in Borneo used to try and bring down the helicopters lifting the wounded out of the jungle, the same way the IRA used to fire over the border in Northern Ireland some years later. I had an Army Air Corps pilot brought in who had been lifting out the padre visiting troops at the front for a week. There were strict rules for take off and landing procedures to try and avoid these problems and he had followed the rules by the book, but sadly the helicopter was hit, killing the padre and badly wounding the pilot. Against all odds he managed to land safely with one arm pretty useless. He had been shot through the shoulder, which was shattered and also shot through the upper lobe of one lung so he was bleeding profusely and short of oxygen. He didn't realise the padre had been killed until he landed and he was devastated.

After primary care we started to rebuild the shoulder again but over the following weeks, as the injuries started to mend, mentally he began to slip into a deep depression. Fellow patients tried to help but without success and he started to see the psychiatrist regularly, with little result as far as I could see. I was getting increasingly concerned that if things didn't improve his career would be threatened. One day treatment by ECT (electroconvulsive therapy) was discussed, which filled me with dread. Luckily something happened which changed the whole scenario – Christmas came.

On Christmas Eve in all military hospitals throughout the world sisters and nurses sang carols around the wards. We would take our corridor capes of grey and scarlet and turn them inside out so that the scarlet was on the outside. Being in Singapore we carried Chinese lanterns on long canes, they looked like copies of the Florence Nightingale lamp, corrugated white paper in a long drum, which held a lighted candle and gave enough light to read our carol sheets. The orderly sergeant of the day would go on ahead of us and extinguish all the overhead and bed lights so the wards were only lit by starlight – no windows above ground level, only blinds to let down in monsoon weather to protect the balcony beds from getting wet.

It was rather a moving procession in the darkened wards and as we entered my ward singing 'Oh come, all ye faithful' something made me hand my lamp to someone and slip away in the dark to stand by the pilot's bed and take his hand. I was thinking, where is this young man in the prime of life going to be next year at this time? Within seconds he started to sob and oh, how he sobbed. That started off the boy in the next bed, then I started and the boy on the other side started. A quick-thinking nurse screened off the bottom of the three beds and we all wept together. For how long, I've no idea. It seemed an eternity but eventually the pilot quietened. There was no sound in the ward, as though everyone was holding their breath, no lights had been put on and then I felt I could slip away, having told him I would arrange for night sister to see that he had something to sleep with. I told night sister and the night orderly what had happened and then I returned to my room.

Next morning was Christmas Day and coming on duty I

wished the night orderly a Happy Christmas and asked how the sergeant was. 'He's fine, Sister.'

'What do you mean, he's fine?'

'Well, he was up at 6 am and made the tea!'

For the first time ever he had made tea for forty patients and delivered it to everyone. I thought that had taken a great deal of courage after what had happened the night before.

From then on he started to really recover and I told the MO to forget the psychiatrist as we were on our way. We eventually sent him up to the Cameron Highlands to convalesce and brought him back for even more intensive physiotherapy on his shoulder and he was returned to his unit in Borneo. In future years I never ever said to my son that 'big boys don't cry' because there are times when big boys have to cry and it's much healthier for them.

The medical officer in charge of my ward was a rather handsome lieutenant commander naval officer who was also our orthopaedic consultant. The uniform in the tropics was all white – shirt, shorts, knee socks and shoes – and I'm still asked by colleagues at reunions if I remember him. He was quite a character as he had been a sick berth attendant before he did medicine and the patients loved him as he had a great affinity with them. An excellent surgeon with sound common sense, he was a real DIY surgeon in theatre and rarely needed the help of his theatre sister – he usually helped himself to the instruments!

One day we had a signal that there had been a nasty accident on one of the aircraft carriers on exercise in the Philippines. A plane landing on the deck hit the arrester wire as usual (it helped with the breaking) and a wheel came off. It shot up the deck and hit two Royal Navy batmen who were on duty guiding the planes in to land, breaking four legs. They were airlifted to the American hospital in Subic Bay for primary care but would be transferred back to us in a couple of days.

They never arrived and I confess I did wonder what their discipline would be like on their return. Our matron at that time was Colonel Priscilla Stewart, an excellent matron but she could be a rather fierce disciplinarian at times and ran a tight ship as they say. She always backed us up and if anyone had complained about her sisters she would have eaten them for breakfast. Colonel Gordon took over some months later and was also an excellent matron.

Nearly three weeks later the commander took a call to say the boys had arrived and were on their way up to the ward in the lift. 'Come on, let's go and meet them,' he said, which was a bit unusual. As the large bed lift clanged to a halt the doors opened and there were the two naval airmen on crutches encased in four enormous plaster of Paris casts from hip to toe, so large in width they couldn't get on pyjamas or uniform trousers so were in what we call modesty pants and boxer shorts. But, each boy had painted on one leg a rather large bare-breasted brown-skinned girl with yellow hair, red lips, yellow grass skirt and a Hawaiian garland of frangipani flowers round her neck. They were painted from knee to ankle and the anatomy of the bosoms had to be seen to be believed. My comment was, 'The Matron will go spare.' The commander of course knew what to expect from the phone call. 'Leave it to me and we'll sort it somehow.' How the boys had mastered swinging their legs on crutches with that enormous weight I'll never know, but they did manage somehow.

On reaching the ward the commander said he was disappearing for about twenty minutes and he would be back. A buzz had gone round the ward and they were queuing up to see 'the girls'. He eventually returned with two very nice maroon terry towelling long dressing gowns – certainly not army issue. He told the boys for Matron and commanding officers' rounds they would wear the dressing gowns with a tight belt round or we would cover the girls with more plaster. Many visitors from the ship came and went – were they charging admission I wondered?

Next morning Matron duly arrived at 11 am to do her round, chatting to the boys about the American hospital and both were very good – 'Yes, Ma'am. No, Ma'am' as appropriate – and we moved on to the next patient. Suddenly out of the corner of my eye I saw them both do a quick 'flash' to the view of the entire opposite row of beds and all the patients went into silent hysteria. Beds appeared to be shaking, sheets were being stuffed in mouths to prevent any laughter issuing forth. My heart sank, she must have seen something and if so I could expect a rocket when the round was over. We continued on and the opposite row of boys were marvellous, their faces deadpan as she spoke to each one in turn and the rest of the ward completely silent. I escorted her to the door of the next ward to hand her over to the other sister – had she a twinkle in her eye? I'm not sure but she disappeared with no comment. I often wondered if she had gone back and told the commanding officer what had happened. Years later, after I had left the QAs, I visited the Cambridge Military Hospital in Aldershot when she was matron in her final year before retirement and she welcomed me like a long lost friend, inviting me to sit next to her at supper. Sadly she is no longer with us but as one of the old school one couldn't help but admire her.

I had a spell of being company commander in Singapore, which was an SRN training school. I had a phone call from the QA orderly officer to say on checking the nurses' quarters at 11 pm there were five nurses missing and they hadn't been seen all day but had all been on days off. I asked the

QA corporal to ring me again at 12 midnight if they hadn't returned. They hadn't, so I contacted the Royal Military Police and asked them to check the streets of downtown Singapore and the clubs, which were very lively at that time of night. They promised to keep looking all night but their mutterings of possible 'white slave traffic to Thailand', in jest or not, was worrying. I had a very restless night but at 7 am the night wardmaster telephoned to say the five nurses had just returned safely, very tired, badly bitten by mosquitoes and sandflies, but otherwise unharmed. What a relief. I'd had visions of headlines in the rag of the times 'QA sister loses five nurses to white slave traffic'.

The girls had taken a sampan – a small local boat being used as a ferry – to an almost uninhabited island to spend the day and have a picnic and had missed the last sampan home. They had to stay in the open all night with only their clothes and towels to protect them. They were a sorry sight, but managed to get the first sampan back. I sent them to have a bath, get into uniform and have breakfast before seeing Matron. Singapore was clear of malaria but mosquitoes could also carry dengue fever and sandfly fever was possible.

Matron and I agreed they had been punished enough and we gave them the rest of the day off and arranged a full medical and necessary treatment. Luckily they made an uneventful recovery but they had learned a hard lesson.

Another holiday Peggy and I had together was a week in Bangkok courtesy of the RAF once more. We stayed in a lovely new hotel in a very pleasant residential area not far from the British Embassy. This was a lovely old colonial building set in beautiful gardens with a very imposing statue of Queen Victoria visible from the road. We had to report there for details of our return flight with the RAF.

Our usual sleep pattern took over most of the week, but the last two days we decided we must see the sights. A crack of dawn awakening to take a tour of the floating market at 6 am. Long flat-bottomed boats carrying all manner of fruit and vegetables stretched along the waterways, sometimes six deep so they stepped from one boat to another. Every so often there were landing stages at various Thai silk factories and shops and we saw Thai silk being spun and woven in the most beautiful iridescent colours. I bought a length in lilac and one in pink and white to have made up into dresses on my return and I still have samples of both. The following day we visited the royal palaces, temples and Buddhas and I have a lovely set of transparencies showing their beautiful colours and designs.

Early in the week we had met two young, courteous and softly spoken American boys about twenty years old who were in Thailand as members of Peace Corps, doing voluntary work for a year. Peggy muttered, 'Don't tell them we're nurses.'

'Certainly not,' I replied. They kept popping up out of the pool by our sunloungers. When it came to asking where we were from Peggy announced we were poodle trimmers from Singapore. A look of incredulity crossed their faces but Peggy carried on. 'Yes, we have a poodle parlour in Singapore.' She kept this up for the week but relented on the last day when we were leaving and saying goodbye and we told them we were army nurses returning to duty!

The flight back was in a Hercules, the plane known as the workhorse of the RAF with a huge belly designed to take a large load of freight. This one was indeed filled with enormous crates secured in the centre and we and the boys sat round the edge of the plane with our backs to the hull. No pressurisation of course but we didn't feel particularly uncomfortable. We had to call at Ubon near the border of Loas to refuel and on landing were greeted with bottles of ice-cold beer; glasses were also supplied for the officers! It went down like nectar. We were able to have a break and freshen up before the last leg of the journey. It was very noisy but we all used sign language and the boys shared fruit and sweets with us the whole way. At Changi we said our thanks and farewells to everyone and got transport back to BMH Singapore ready for the fray once more.

During 1964 we had local riots carried out by the Indian Communists and they were very unpleasant. Cars full of people would be rocked and overturned, set alight burning people to death. They used Molotov cocktails which are incendiary devices, bottles filled with petrol containing a wick which is lit and when thrown explodes on impact, setting fire to anything near it. This went on and off for several months and curfews would be in operation when one could only leave home to buy food and necessities between 6 am and 9 am. We had a wedding in the mess when one of our sisters married a Royal Fleet Auxiliary captain at 8 am and then had a dash to the Singapore-Malayan Causeway before 9 am to get away on honeymoon. The reception had to be cancelled and rebooked for when they came back again. We were eating the food for days! I also remember going to catch an early morning plane at RAF Changi with an armed escort but all we saw were a few stray dogs.

A lull in the troubles gave me a rare weekend off and with no curfew I invited a boyfriend off one of the aircraft carriers to go to Singapore Swimming Club to which most of us belonged. It was a pleasant day off there and one could have lunch by the pool.

I drove north from the hospital in Alexandra to the naval base to pick him up and then took a road going south east I hadn't been down before. The club was by the sea but we were forbidden to swim in the sea because of cholera. Halfway across the island we were suddenly in a recent riot area with debris of burnt-out cars, remnants of incendiary devices and a terrible smell, which could only mean burned bodies. There was a Malay Army checkpoint and although we were not in uniform we both had service ID cards so we were allowed to go on our way. We arrived safely, changed and settled down to our first iced coffee – a speciality of the house. A tall glass filled with iced coffee and a dollop of vanilla ice cream on the top – delicious! It cost 2/6d (two shillings and sixpence) and was worth every penny.

We hadn't been there very long, it was about 11.30 am, when over the tannoy we were told that the curfew was coming down again at 1 pm and would we please go home. We changed again and went to the car. I suddenly said, 'You drive!' and threw him the keys and we joined the throng of cars and people making their way along the south coast towards Keppel Harbour and the town centre. Total chaos as banks, businesses and shops all turned out to join the queue to get home; pretty well stop/start all the way. Eventually we were through the town and on the main road to Alexandra and then we found ourselves going through another Indian quarter and in the middle of a riot.

The boyfriend was concentrating hard trying not to run over the rioters, avoiding flying Molotov's and moving forward very, very slowly; the next minute there were eight pairs of hands on the window sills of the car – all open of course in that heat. I thought, 'Well, this is it, we are going to die and mum and dad won't know what has happened,' which was a bit daft as they would find out soon enough. I don't think either of us showed any fear as such as we were both concentrating on other things. After a few minutes when I was expecting hands to start rocking the car I realised that eight pairs of hands were gently moving the car forward and making no attempt to interfere with us at all. All rather strange, I thought. After what seemed like a long time we were through the quarter and driving down the open road as fast as we could as it was nearly 1 pm and he had to get transport back to the naval base.

When we arrived back at Alexandra, Matron was in uniform on the hospital steps and came down to meet us. 'Are you both alright?'

'Yes, we are fine but it's a bit hairy down there,' was my reply. I introduced her to the boyfriend and she told him to go and see the naval wardmaster for transport. She told me to get into uniform and return on duty. I can't remember saying goodbye to the boyfriend and I never saw him again – I think he thought it a bit dodgy going out with Margaret Madin!

There were times in the next few weeks when I asked

myself, why didn't they kill us? I can't remember ever telling Matron or colleagues what had happened to us, we were too busy with other casualties. Then one day in a quiet moment a memory of an incident came back to me, which I had forgotten about. When Yvonne was posted to Nepal I took over her room as it had a telephone in it for theatre calls. I also took over her amah who was new to me – they did the work of a batwoman at home. One afternoon the amah stood in the doorway with my clean laundry when I had just woken up from a sleep.

'Missy wear sari?'

'No,' I replied.

'Missy *never* wear sari?'

'No,' I replied and was thinking why should I wear a sari, but I was still befuddled with sleep and never asked her why I should wear a sari. Then things began to click into place. I was very tanned from R&R, I had dark hair piled up on top of my head – she must have thought I was Indian.

Another odd incident happened not long before I left for home. Returning to theatre after lunch one day I idly picked up the notes of the first patient on the list and read Bin Madin on the cover, which meant wife of a Ghurkha Madin. I really thought the theatre boys were up to their tricks and had put me on the afternoon's gynae list, but opening the cover it was a genuine patient. I had never in two years service ever seen my name before on any notes. I called my Malay sergeant and asked what is the Malay translation of the name Madin; he looked at me rather strangely and said 'Son of Mohammed'. So it would appear the locals thought I was a Muslim as well as Indian! The boyfriend hadn't been blonde and blue eyed but tanned from three months at sea, dark hair, hazel eyes. I think that is why we survived the riot. They thought we were Indians.

I was getting to the end of my two years but I have memories of three patients in that orthopaedic ward who must have been glad to come under the hands of the commander. A Ghurkha soldier was brought in from Borneo with a terrible hand injury from a grenade exploding in or very near his hand. The patient's notes said 'for amputation'. The remains of the hand was just a mushy pulp and unrecognisable but the commander wasn't into amputations. I was told, for some reason which I failed to understand with these marvellous brave men, that there was some 'loss of face' with the loss of limbs. Over the following weeks the commander fashioned a replica thumb and finger with bone and skin grafts from this mess, which would enable the Ghurkha to lift a glass or cup and hold a certain amount of things, who on his discharge would be returned to Nepal. Another hand injury was an army sergeant who was riding a motorbike on a Malayan road; he rode round a corner and slap bang into a fire engine, which was driving on the wrong side of the road. He held onto the bike and was tossed into the undergrowth but the throttle lever did terrible damage right down to the bones of the wrist. Grass, soil and all sorts of debris was impacted into the hand. I can see the commander now talking to the soldier and gently picking out the grass at the bedside and the soldier not even being aware of what he was doing.

'We'll soon fix you up,' he said and he did. Bones and dislocated fingers were thoroughly cleaned and put back in line and he eventually returned to duty with a repaired and reconstructed hand.

The third case was a big strapping marine sergeant who came out of the jungle with a slipped disc. A laminectomy could be quite a serious operation on the spine and I expected him to be evacuated to UK to convalesce with perhaps a lighter job for a time. These men were incredibly fit and at eight weeks he was back in Borneo – if I hadn't been witness to it I'm not sure I would have believed it.

In October 1965 I was to return home to my family which I was looking forward to but in later years I was to look back on these two years as the happiest in my professional life and be eternally grateful that the Queen Elizabeth Hospital had trained me so well that I managed to cope with whatever the British Army had thrown at me.

I was never to work at such pressure again – the rest of my time would seem to be a doddle.

It was lovely to see my family again after two years but it was a strange feeling now that the adrenaline had stopped running and I felt a bit lost at times. It turned out to be quite a hard winter and we had snow at the end of November and into December. My father was nearing seventy-five years and, as 'one of the old school' regarding snow clearing, had insisted on tackling the steps leading down to the garage, even though we had a very good handrail. There had been a heavy snowfall the night before and I begged him to stop as he was attempting too much. That night he had a stroke and died peacefully in hospital ten days later but at least having been abroad off and on for eight years I was in the right place at the right time to help my mother, for which I was truly thankful.

I was to miss my father a great deal over the years. My sister and I had been brought up in a relatively strict Victorian household and as a WWI acting sergeant major when father said 'jump' we all 'jumped'. I found him a gentle, kind man, who would help anyone in trouble; he had endless patience with me wanting to know how everything worked. We were constantly told to use one's common sense when making decisions and often used that WWI saying regarding shells. 'If your name is on it, it will get you, so don't worry about it', which took me through some hairy moments in the QAs, as it had taken him through two world wars with narrow escapes. He had prepared me well, if unknowingly, for a strict nurse training and sixteen years in the QAs. I'm only sorry my son will never know his Grandpa. In January 1966 my next posting was to be to the Millbank Military Hospital next door to the Tate Gallery and very central for shopping and theatres.

9

London

January 1966 – December 1968

The military hospital at Millbank was a very specialised hospital dealing mainly in cancer and leukaemia cases. We worked alongside Westminster Hospital for the radiotherapy side of it, useful because it was just down the road. Chemotherapy wasn't a word I'd heard of at that time. The Guards regiments doing royal guard duties were also catered for in dentals and ENT but anything else plus emergency cases were all sent to the Royal Herbert Hospital, Woolwich.

I was on night duty pretty quickly after my arrival and then on 19th February I was to relieve Yvonne in theatre at Woolwich. She had saved up all her leave and was off to South Africa to spend six weeks with her sister and brother-in-law, who had a fruit farm. I was very interested to see the Royal Herbert as my father had spoken of it. After three years in the trenches he had been sent back to the gunners depot to break in new horses for the regiment and then to become an officer cadet. I have a lovely photograph of him mounted on his horse, immaculate in turn out of uniform with the white band round his peaked cap. They wanted him to join the cavalry and go to India but the war ended and he was expected to return home to Grandpa and take up cabinet making again which he had left in 1914. He once told me I might have been born in India, a strange coincidence.

I enjoyed those weeks in Woolwich with a good variety of surgery and everyone so welcoming when one went on relief duties. We had trips to London on days off and they introduced me to the best eating houses in Blackheath. The hospital seemed to have changed little since it had been opened by Queen Victoria in 1865 – long Nightingale wards similar to Colchester with iron stoves which heated the wards in the past and stove pipes going up to the roof still in place. Central heating was now used of course and the stoves would be used to display flowers for CO's inspection once a fortnight. A long tradition I found in Colchester was for one of the patients to ask me if I would like some flowers. 'That would be very nice,' I would say. Two nights before, up-patients would go and do a 'recce' of the CO's garden and then the night before the boys would go and pick flowers after dark! The flowers would arrive in a bucket of water by my desk and I would arrange them in a large display on the stove and the CO would admire them on passing, but no questions asked, no names, no pack-drill. Although we all knew where they had come from, the CO's eyes would twinkle.

In April I went into theatre at Millbank as one of the team. Dentals and ENT I was at home with, cancer cases were very new to me and a steep learning curve. That first year we lost three sisters to cancer (one of whom I had trained with at QEH), which was very distressing. All had appeared to ignore warning signs and I had seen a surgeon in tears when opening up a colleague of twenty years and finding he could do nothing for her. It was a time when symptoms of cancer were not talked about, thankfully all that has now changed.

Millbank was run very much as a hospice although Dame Cicely Saunders did not open her first hospice until 1967. There was very open visiting when convenient for the relatives and friends; certainly some pain control; if patients were fit to travel then they could go home every weekend when treatments were finished at the Westminster Hospital. From all over the world anyone diagnosed or suspected of possibly having cancer would be sent back to Millbank and when invited to do so, visiting consultants from the London hospitals would pop in to help with diagnosis and possible treatments. Sometimes they would come and help with operations and many different needles and sutures were kept sterile and ready and made it interesting surgery. There were only a few 'atraumatic' sutures then, usually for intestinal and eye work. These had the suture punched onto a needle with no eye to cause damage going through the delicate tissues.

I had been home whenever I could at weekends but I decided I needed a break in June, I seemed to be mentally exhausted. I booked two weeks in a five-star hotel in Torremolinos (£84 full board for two weeks!). It was still very much a fishing village in those days although large new hotels were beginning to appear. I met two very nice holiday reps on the plane also going for two weeks holiday and we all met up sometimes in the evening to go and watch flamenco dancing or go on a night tour to various places. In those days it always felt safe walking home alone in the early hours with lots of families about. I think I was a bit suspect in the hotel, as a single woman staying alone was unusual, but they seemed to get used to me. My passport said 'civil servant' now instead of 'army nursing sister' as it used to be before travelling in civilian clothes. I made a big effort and booked tours from the hotel on alternate days in the week. The Red Cross had filled the bottom of my case with a selection of paperbacks in case I didn't speak to a soul for two weeks! Strangely, when I took a few down to the pool they became a talking point and people would ask to borrow them. I went to Grenada and to see the Alhambra, very lovely. This entailed a very early start as I remember, but a lovely journey through the mountains going north. I had another lovely day in Gibraltar with a Red Cross welfare officer I had known in Iserlohn who was at the Royal Naval Hospital. We had lunch there and then did the sights including, of course, up the Rock to see the mischievous apes. It was very British, with familiar policemen, red post boxes and telephone boxes; I could have been in London.

Back in the hotel, the Tres Cabaleros, I was always invited to join a table of eight for dinner in the evenings, some of whom were ex-service families. We took it in turn to buy the wine and the extra strawberries that were on the menu. One retired naval officer farmed in Lincolnshire, the Birds Eye 'surprise peas' – tiny, very sweet peas frozen on the night immediately after being harvested and advertised regularly on the TV with an eye-catching few minutes. It was very pleasant with excellent company and I returned fully refreshed to Millbank having not read half of the paperbacks but having had a most enjoyable holiday.

In August I was promoted to major with drinks all round in the mess but no more night duty for me. In November I was told I was to lead the London contingent of QAs for the Festival of Remembrance held each year at the Royal Albert Hall and this was to be a very interesting London experience.

We had to report at the Royal Albert Hall early Friday morning to the Guards regimental sergeant major who was to be in charge of the parade. People with little knowledge of marching had rehearsed earlier in the week. We spent the morning marching up and down the first flight of stairs. It really was quite frightening at first, as we had to look ahead holding our heads up high and not look down at our feet or the steps. Half way down another tier began so the step was longer than usual and almost guaranteed to throw you and your other half out of step if your step length was different. After lunch we marched down the steps and across the arena, then up another flight to find the correct seat reserved for us on the platform. It was pointed out by the regimental sergeant major that if one took the wrong seat it could throw the entire parade out, which wasn't exactly a boost for one's morale. On Saturday it was repeated many times and we were really getting very tired. We had a longer lunch break and in the late afternoon a dress rehearsal for an invited audience which was rather nice.

Evening came and we all lined up in our places along the corridor running round the outside of the arena. We followed the Guards so we were lined up alongside them.

We had a soft spot for them as when in hospital they always finished up asking if they could 'bull' our heavy shoes (our beetle crushers, as we used to call them). They would sit for hours with a bit of shiny bone polishing our shoes with spit and polish so that you could see your face in them; they lasted for ages with just a rub up.

I think we were all rather glad that this was going to be the last time we marched down those stairs. The guardsmen, tall in their bearskins, had just been given the command to come to attention prior to marching off when the guardsman beside me dug his mate in the ribs with his elbow saying, 'If you don't watch it, mate, you'll be arse over tip down those stairs – begging your pardon, ma'am,' and was gone. All the QAs were reduced to hysterics and I'm not sure how we got down the stairs but we all had a smile on our faces. We felt if the Guards thought it was not that easy why should we nurses worry too much. We arrived safely in our seats and settled down to enjoy the rest of the evening's entertainment and then the very moving Service of Remembrance and those millions of poppies coming down on our heads. My only thoughts were of my father's comrades from WWI.

That Christmas of 1966 I asked Matron if my mother could come as a guest and stay for Christmas and she readily agreed. We always had the choice of working either Christmas or New Year. Mum came for four days and thoroughly enjoyed her stay. She had breakfast in bed much to her surprise and then the Red Cross girls invited her to help in the department organising the Christmas presents for the remaining sick patients and that kept her occupied most of the day. She enjoyed the food, the company and the excitement in the hospital, getting organised for Father Christmas doing his rounds. It was quite a tonic for her after all the trauma of my father's death the previous Christmas. Whenever I came back from leave afterwards she would send a large box of Thorntons toffee for the maids who looked after her. She had never met any people of colour before and was overwhelmed by the kindness shown to her.

In February 1967 I took over theatre as two senior majors had moved on to higher things. Clare had returned to the UK from Singapore a year before me as her father had died suddenly and her mother, who was crippled with arthritis, needed more help. Clare had another VIP trip back by escorting a Ghurkha by sea for an operation at the Chest Hospital in Hindhead. She travelled by Blue Funnel Line (out of Liverpool) and met her husband to be, who was the catering officer on board. She was posted to Millbank as a compassionate posting and possibly the first QA to marry and be allowed to stay in the corps as Dom disappeared for a six-month voyage to Australia as was usual in the merchant navy. On Corps Day in March we celebrated with a church service, drinks and lunch in the mess and Clare invited her brother and friend on leave from P&O. I was introduced to my husband to be along with the rest of the party but thought little of the event at the time.

In June I was told I was to be on duty for Her Majesty at the Queen's birthday parade of Trooping the Colour, which was an exciting thought. We had a full dress rehearsal the Saturday before and I was shown the small room set aside with a couch and pretty soft peach blankets. Her Majesty rode side-saddle in those days in the uniform of Colonel-in-Chief Grenadier Guards and was as competent a rider as any on parade so I didn't anticipate any problems and looked forward to enjoying the day. As usual it was a very warm summer day and a superb parade. No one can do pageantry like the British Army and I can still get a lump in my throat when I hear the slow march to 'Skipio' and 'Les Huguenots'. That duty was a chance in a lifetime and I will never forget it. I was now into my second year of doing very little else but cancer surgery and I found it very depressing. All my service life I had been seeing my patients get well and I was missing the patients very much. My cases came to me in theatre already asleep and went out asleep. My seniority meant that I would be getting into administration in the future and I began to think seriously about leaving the QAs. Suddenly Matron sent for me and asked me to go as her representative to a finance meeting at one of the old London banks. At that meeting I sat next to Lt. Col. Hunt QARANC from MOD. At the tea and biscuits stage she said there were two nice postings coming up in the New Year in the Recruiting and Liaison Organisation, one at HQ Southern Command in Wiltshire and one at HQ Western Command in Chester and would I be interested? Matron-in-Chief, Brigadier Gordon, my old matron from Singapore had agreed I should be approached in this matter. Was this an answer to a prayer? I knew nothing about the job description but if Brig. Gordon thought I could do it it was worth giving it some thought. I asked if I could think about it and meanwhile would they please not tell my matron! I don't know what made me say that but when she eventually had my posting order in her hand she was not best pleased. It would be a complete change of environment and it could be the answer to my problems. I chose Chester as it was nearer to home and where I had been for my first interview. Clare and husband were moving to just outside Chester and it would be nice to know someone up there. Not a word leaked about my decision and meanwhile I carried on as usual. When the posting order came in Matron was so cross she threw the paper across the desk saying, 'And what do you think of that?' I read it through carefully thinking how I was going to reply, as she had obviously not heard a whisper about it.

'Well, ma'am, it will be different won't it?' and I was dismissed.

The weekend of the Lord Mayor's Show in November I began to feel distinctly unwell. Earlier in the week I'd had some intensive dental work carried out and unfortunately I went down with a massive mouth infection. The mouth is full of dirty old bugs and if you get below par it can hit you. We had been short of staff, working overtime and struggling to get days off.

I was admitted to Barry Ward on the Monday after seeing the dental consultant and put on an antibiotic for the fungal infection but no penicillin. I was there for ten days living on porridge, milk puddings and two hourly Milo as I couldn't tolerate anything else. At the start of the second week I was still having very high temperatures when one night I went through what I recognise now as the old fashioned 'crisis' from the days before penicillin. Very interesting from a nursing point of view, the walls of the room and the furniture all seemed to be closing in and trying to crush me as in a nightmare and it was extremely frightening. I suddenly woke up and looked at the clock and it said 3.45 am. I rang the bell for Sister and asked her if she would take my temperature as my head had cleared and I felt better. It had dropped from nearly 104° to 99° and the crisis was over, I was back in the land of the living but was not a pretty sight with black scabs all over my lips, which were also signs of old pneumonia cases but I had *not* had any chest infection at all.

The next day Matron asked me if I would like to go home or to the Osborne House Convalescent Home for Officers on the Isle of White. I opted for Osborne as it had a high reputation for getting one back on one's feet quickly. This was the Wednesday and they found me a place for Friday. There was a strict dress code at Osborne, trousers were allowed in the day because of the various activities but after 6 pm gentlemen had to wear suits and ladies dresses (no blouses and skirts).

On the Thursday I was up and dressed for the first time, feeling very fragile. I had to get my hair done and also buy slacks and another dress as I was there for two weeks. A friend kindly escorted me to the shops. On the Friday afternoon I had a taxi to the boat train to Southampton and then across on the ferry to East Cowes where the Osborne Rolls Royce picked up the five convalescents for the journey to the house and I must admit I and the other four officers looked very poorly.

The three services took it in turns to appoint a high ranking medical officer for five years to be in charge and this time it was the turn of the navy. On arrival we all had to be medically examined by the admiral. He read my history and just couldn't believe I had no sign of pneumonia. My mouth was still sore and the black scabs on my lips would bleed easily – embarrassing at the table when I would have to excuse myself in the first few days. He was horrified to find I had been up for the first time the day before and promptly cancelled the usually obligatory physiotherapy at 9.30 am each morning. One was not allowed breakfast in bed but one was allowed to rest in the afternoon which I made full use of the first week.

There was a resident physiotherapist, remedial gymnast and an occupational therapist all very highly trained to get us fit and back on duty with very well-equipped departments. Occupational therapy was obligatory for all at 10.45 am and we had our 'naafi break' there with coffee and biscuits organised in the department. Soft music of the classical sort was in the background, which I found very relaxing. You could play table tennis, billiards, the piano, do carpentry and bookbinding and I decided to learn tapestry, which I had never done before. I chose a lovely old Jacobean design which I would have made up into a fire screen-cum-coffee table and which I still use to this day.

After lunch there were many activities available to get one out and about as one's health improved. Queen Victoria had her own private beach and you could walk, swim or sail depending on the weather. The gardens were lovely and held the children's fort where they had drilled playing soldiers and a lovely big play house – super 'Wendy' house to us. One could also play golf, croquet or bowls.

There was also a shooting range, which brought back memories untold of Ghana. Major Bokenham, the matron in Ghana, had somehow persuaded me to accompany her to an all-female shooting class, which was run by the army for wives, teachers and anyone attached to the units. I luckily paid a joining fee before we started, although not pressed to do so – perhaps people gave up after the first class. I explained to the sergeant that I had never held a gun in my life and he was very good at assuming I could be an idiot. I carried out his instructions to the letter, not knowing it was competition day; I had the highest score and walked away with a small silver spoon with crossed rifles, which I still have. Pure beginner's luck but some of the other ladies were not very happy. I went twice more so as not to lose face and then never went again.

I did go to the firing range at Osborne as one of our group, a lieutenant commander wanted some company. It was now December and bitterly cold and lying prone and leaning over sandbags I was very glad of my old sheepskin jacket from days in Germany. The next morning we woke up to a white over with a fall of snow. One of the sisters (all civilian) was an Australian and had never seen snow before and was so excited we had to stop her rolling in it but we taught her how to snowball and build a snowman!

By the second week our party was looking a great deal better. All my black crusts had separated and I was looking more like my normal self and getting more energy, not needing sleep in the afternoon. The dining room staff were wonderful, never forgetting my soft diet and asking me if I would like the dish prepared for me. All the food was very good. I would have to be careful of hot liquids for the rest of my life, as some nerve damage had been done to my lips but a small price to pay to be well again.

One afternoon a guide was arranged to escort a large party of us round the closed part of the house for a viewing of the royal private apartments, which were only open in the summer. A most interesting visit, beautiful furniture, Persian carpets, portraits and landscapes all to admire. The royal bedroom was slightly morbid, left just as it was on the day Albert died, rather like a shrine.

Two weeks had gone by and it was time for our group to return to duty. The motley crew which arrived in various hues of the grey of sickness had all disappeared and in its place were five officers of good colour, bright eyed and alert getting into the Rolls Royce to return to the ferry at East Cowes. We would never meet again but I was so pleased to have experienced Osborne, for the kindness of fellow officers and the help of all the professionals to get us back on our feet again.

In January I would be taking up the appointment of women's services liaison officer in the Recruiting and Liaison branch of the Ministry of Defence at HQ Western Command at Chester.

10

Chester

January 1968 – January 1972

I was to be the new women's services liaison officer at HQ Westerm Command in Chester, taking over from Rosemary Martin who was finishing her two years tour of duty. The Recruiting and Liaison branch consisted of a full colonel, a lieutenant colonel, a retired brigadier and a major WRAC and myself, all sharing an office and all the schools work and a lovely lady in charge of the typing pool, Mrs Fraser, who looked after us all. We all got on well and I found it a very happy unit.

I was responsible for encouraging suitable girls and qualified nurses to think of the QAs as a possible career. There was a national shortage of nurses so hospitals were very keen to keep hold of their qualified staff and we were well understaffed for sisters ourselves. We had a two-year waiting list for girls wishing to train as state registered nurses but recruits for state enrolled nurses (the practical bedside nurse) could be enlisted fairly quickly along with dental hygienists, medical clerks and later on ward assistants. In

1970 we needed two hundred and thirty more sisters.

The military hospitals were recognised and inspected by the General Nursing Council and we followed the GNC curriculum. Potential SRNs joined for four years since it had to include embarkation and disembarkation leave as part of their training was done overseas. Our main work was visiting schools of all types from independent (private) schools to the secondary modern schools, as they were known at the time, colleges of further education, as many had pre-nursing courses, and hospitals to speak to third- or fourth-year nurses when invited to do so. We were very much involved with career conventions at which we gave advice on subjects to take from the school choices and spoke to the parents who were very interested in the welfare and discipline side of our care for the girls at home and abroad. It was a great advantage being a fairly senior officer who had been a company commander and I had this information at my finger tips to reassure parents.

We covered Lancashire, Cheshire, Shropshire, Staffordshire, Warwickshire, Worcestershire and the whole of Wales, which was fifteen thousand square miles and they first of all gave us a Mini and later on a Morris Traveller, which was much more suitable for carrying the projector and equipment.

Rosemary and I had a week for handover and she

showed me the drill for schools and I met several careers officers at Youth Employment Bureaux with whom we worked quite closely. Sharing the office with Sue Richards was a distinct advantage as she had been with the army team of lecturers so was familiar with all the problems, she could also have written a good food guide along with a good loo guide where we could change into uniform on long journeys – most of these places were in lovely country pubs full of gentleman farmers.

Sue was particularly helpful to me with writing letters. I was only used to writing letters to Matron in the official format of 'Madam, I have the honour to request –' when asking for leave, going on a course, asking for a posting etc. and finishing 'I have the honour to be, Madam, Your obedient servant' followed by my name, rank and number. The writing of letters to schools requesting that one might call to introduce oneself or give a talk and film in their careers programme had to be particularly tactful as some council areas were anti-army. At this time the convents, if giving *any* careers information, would only consider nursing and teaching professions as suitable for their girls so I found myself doing most of the convents particularly in Liverpool, of which there were many. Areas like Toxteth, Croxteth, Scotland Road, I've done them all.

With being WRAC Sue was accommodated at Saighton

Camp Chester but we were in the officers' mess RAF Sealand, seven miles up the Queensferry Road along with 2nd Officer Shelagh Phillips WRNS and Fl. Officer Lyn Walters WRAF. Shelagh was a recruiter at their office in Liverpool and Lyn at the RAF Recruiting Office in Wrexham. We would sometimes meet up at tri-service talks and fairly often at careers conventions. Neither of them had the huge area I covered. It was nice to have female company in a predominantly male mess and coming home late at night from conventions, say in Blackpool, three tri-service Minis would leave in convoy and if we could hit the first traffic light at green entering Liverpool we could travel non-stop through nine more and then quickly through The Mersey Tunnel to Birkenhead. We kept doors and windows locked and never lost sight of one another. It would sometimes be after 11 pm and if we hadn't had a decent meal at the school we would stop at the Little Chef opposite the gates of RAF Sealand for a good mixed grill before heading for bed.

The biggest worry in the first year was actually finding one's way to the school. Sue's knowledge of good routes to schools was invaluable. Routes had to be worked out with approximate timing plus half an hour in case of roadworks and it usually worked well. Nearing the areas, signs for schools, garages and women pushing prams were the most reliable for giving directions. The only motorway there was in my area was the M6 and I didn't use it all that often as bad weather, fog or rain round Warrington made it notorious for accidents. A Mini sandwiched between enormous lorries almost in your boot was not my cup of tea and I would get off the M6 at the first opportunity and drive the long way but safer way home.

We had quite a heavily booked year and further requests would come in by telephone. A request was made to MOD for QA uniform and it was passed to me and I attended a marvellous 'Nursing through the Ages' pageant organised by the principle nurse tutor of Llandudno General Hospital showing nurses through from Roman times to the present day. The beautiful and authentic costumes were all made by the hospital sewing staff, many scenes were quite breathtaking with the colours and richness of the dresses. I went as myself and word soon flashed round that I was the genuine article! The aim was a recruiting drive and I was met with much kindness and great interest of the Scarlet and Grey and they very generously asked me to be the first on stage for the present day finale. An imaginary meeting between Charles Dickens, Sarah Gamp and Florence Nightingale was hilarious with Sarah whacking Florence over the head with the brolly. The Brownies, Cubs, Scouts and Guides in the audience just loved it! It was a great privilege to have been invited to take part in this excellent presentation to packed houses of the theatres in Rhyl, Denbigh, Llandudno and Bangor on four different evenings. The production was produced by Mrs Tasker Jones a well-known figure in North Wales.

In June Shelagh organised a familiarization visit for all of us to RN Air Station Brawdy South West Wales to speak to the WRNS. Twenty-eight out of the twenty-nine trades were working there. Between us we could provide about forty trades for girls from leaving school with no CSEs going through to girls with two A Levels for officer entry. Some of the trades were duplicated like stewardess, catering, secretaries, stores, drivers etc. but each service had some trades unique to them. WRAC had kennel maid and groom, radar operator and musician. The WRNS and WRAF had air mechanics, radio operator, radar plotter, weapons analyst, and of course the nurses from all three services.

I was astonished at the confidence the pilots of these planes (worth over a million pounds then) had in the highly skilled aircraft mechanics who serviced and checked the aircraft. When busy chatting to one of the WRNS the pilot walked to his plane, gave a thumbs up to the girl who gave a thumbs up back and he got in and took off, I had much admiration for both of them. We stirred the curiosity of the naval officers with our three different uniforms and we left them in no doubt as to who we were and the job we were doing for all three services. A very enjoyable and informative packed thirty-six hours at Brawdy.

In August I was sent to the Army School of Education at Beaconsfield for the one-week projectionists course. As the army carried Bell and Howell projectors this was most welcome and very good. There were times at schools when the projectionist wasn't quite sure what he was doing and could damage the film. I was horrified to find my own 'Challenge and Reward' film was damaged with torn sprockets, three burns and very bad scratches. We learned how to take the projector to pieces and then put it back together, then at lunch time the instructor would sneakily remove bulbs and fuses and at 2 pm tell us to find out what was wrong, as it wouldn't work. By the end of the week we were very proficient at finding out what was wrong and putting it right.

Living in the newly opened officer's mess was an education in itself. Living quarters were on the fifteenth floor of a skyscraper block and the rooms were well furnished and pleasantly designed. A covered way led to a spacious anteroom, dining room and general amenities, all set in lovely grounds.

The only other female in the mess was Capt. Liz

Simmons WRAC who kindly took me under her wing and introduced me to many interesting service and civilian personnel. Within the week she had persuaded me to do Scottish country dancing and thirty games of tennis in an American tournament in which all members of the unit took part including the WRAC girls. I enjoyed seeing the girls in their jobs I had been lecturing about for six months and had long chats with the cooks and stewardesses in the mess.

Mess members consisted of officers from Nepal, Ghana and several Middle Eastern countries learning English, naval reserve officers brushing up on Russian, British officers learning Arabic and one Japanese gentleman from Tokyo learning Russian through English; and I struggle with English! It was a very educational and happy visit from many points of view.

In the August of 1967 I had started going out with Clare's brother Alan and in the autumn of '68 we were engaged and planned to marry on his next leave from P&O in March '69. As Alan would be returning to sea for either a four-and-a-half-month or six-month tour I was another sister allowed to marry and stay in the corps and in the job, which was good for continuity for the next few years as there was a lot to learn.

We had regular attendances at recruiting conferences

either at MOD or locally where we were brought up to date with numbers required and enjoyed meeting WSLOs from other parts of the country such as Scotland and Northern Ireland. Annually we had a joint services headmistresses conference in Westminster, which certainly impressed the headmistresses as many invitations to schools and to interview girls came in afterwards and they always mentioned how much they had enjoyed it. We would host a reception at the RAF Club Piccadilly the evening before the conference for everyone to meet. The male officers would be in mess kit making it a pleasant, colourful evening for the headmistresses, which may well have contributed to their enjoyment. The services know how to entertain.

Career conventions were sometimes held in large halls and not in the schools and a memorable one was at the Benn Memorial Hall in Rugby where we were located next to the hotel and catering stand. It was an exhausting day with lots of brochure hunters and a terrible noise only made bearable by the cooking demonstrations next door. The hotel and catering stand slipped us hot crêpe suzettes and Cona coffee laced with brandy at regular intervals to eat and drink behind the screens! We all received a good meal before the evening session.

In March of '69 we gave a careers presentation at Cardiff Castle to the directors of education covering the whole command, which was another good day. Sue and I had to address this august audience and tell of the opportunities for girls. We also had chosen members of the army giving their own stories of how they had progressed and they were all excellent. One memorable one was a regimental sergeant major who told how he had come from the back streets of Dublin with little education to join the British Army. He managed to pass the recruiting office test and worked his way up slowly, with army classes along the way. With his first stripe he managed to buy a bicycle, a second stripe a motorbike, a third stripe a first car and now as an RSM he had become a member of a posh golf club in Surrey and had an Aston Martin parked outside in the castle car park for all to see. His delivery was marvellous and he brought the house down.

In June '69 we had a very large ARMEX (Army Exhibition) at Belle Vue Manchester covering four days. This was first class and if it didn't bring in the recruits it wasn't for lack of trying. Major Margaret McDermott (WSLO Northern Command), myself and two trained SENs from Catterick Military Hospital dealt with over eighty genuine enquiries for the QAs. We were all in indoor uniform attracting other visitors to the stand which included three ex-RAMC, four ex-patients, eight ex-QAs, nurses and sisters, one seventy-five-year-old who serenaded us with a squeeze box for ten minutes, one drunk looking for QA literature to read in bed, one elderly lady of seventy-four for a chat about the Army Catering Corps who had given her a free omelette and piece of gateau which made her day. We resuscitated at least twenty people after watching simulated operations by TA RAMC in 'Emergency Ward 10' next door to us. It was a pretty exhausting four days but we all hoped productive. We all asked if anyone had a spare pair of feet.

That year I also attended the public speaking course for liaison officers at the Army School of Recruiting in Woolwich. The course was taken by a Professor Holgate whose speciality was the works of William Shakespeare. He was very pro QAs as he had been a patient in a military hospital. We had been told to prepare to deliver a ten-minute talk to the class on the first day. We would have to deliver a piece of prose and also be involved outside in 'Opening a Fête' during our time in class. I have no memorabilia of this course, which is unusual, so these are really thirty-year-old memories.

My prepared talk to the class was 'Macau on a Shoestring'. On the final Friday of one of my Hong Kong visits I decided to go and see the garden city of Macau. I hadn't many HK dollars left as I was returning to Singapore the next day. I had purchased what I thought was a return ticket on the hydrofoil as I'm not a good sailor and it took much less time than the ferry. On arrival at Macau I was told it was only a single so I immediately had to spend half my dollars on a return ticket, which left me with something like twenty to twenty-five dollars (a HK dollar was equivalent to one shilling and four pence).

Standing on the quay was a tour bus for the day, much too expensive, a taxi, also too expensive. I stood there thinking I would have to walk round in the heat when a voice at my elbow said, 'Missy, see Macau?' It was a pedicab driver, a pedicab is a rickshaw attached to a bicycle that also has a hood for shade.

'How much?'

'Ten dollars for the day.'

'Yes please.' He was a super young man and a great tourist guide and in a pleasant, leisurely way took me all round Macau.

Macau was part of mainland China but had been Portuguese since a treaty with China in 1557. I saw lovely buildings, monuments, temples, a memorable façade of the remains of St. Paul's Church standing alone at the top of a flight of steps. Before lunch I was taken to one of the two casinos. Yes, it was open and I could go inside for free. It was like stepping into a James Bond film, deep red plush carpets, enormous chandeliers all lit up, people already playing at the tables – no charge to look round. Fascinating.

For lunch he took me to a small family-run café, almost empty at that time but they produced a perfect minute steak with vegetables, a drink and fruit for about six HK dollars. It couldn't have been nicer. After lunch we continued seeing lovely gardens in cool resting places and he then took me back to catch the afternoon hydrofoil. I tipped him my few remaining dollars, thanked him for his kindness and returned to Hong Kong with a few cents to catch the bus back up Nathan Road, having had a much nicer day seeing 'Macau on a shoestring'.

For my piece of prose I chose 'The Parable of the Good Samaritan' from St. Luke's Gospel, which I delivered from the pulpit of a packed Garrison Church in Rheindahlen for QA Day in Germany in 1962 so it was already well prepared. Using my sergeant major voice I had little trouble opening the fête in the gardens and making myself heard to the professor who seemed to be a very long way away. Having already been speaking to schools for over a year I found the rest of the course relatively easy, yes, a talk must have a beginning, a middle and an end which I had found out the hard way but it was a pleasant two weeks.

In the school summer holiday we caught up with filling in the card index system with all our visits to the schools over the past year. The office was peaceful and the telephone rarely rang, it was impossible to do this at any other time of the year.

In July 1969 I realised I had only interviewed one potential officer in the eighteen months I had been in the job. I knew how desperately short of sisters we were and we also recruited non nursing officers for administrative duties. Whatever the system was it didn't seem to be working. I wrote to every women's service careers officer (usually WRAC) at all the recruiting offices in the command informing them of my wish to meet all interested personnel for an informal interview. The staff nurses would only visit on their days off or on holiday, as they would not wish their hospitals to know they were making enquiries. It started slowly at first with the one girl to interview and then gradually I found I was interviewing three to five girls during the morning. Sometimes friends would come together to the recruiting office where I met them.

The professional competence of the girl would be assessed by the commissioning board but I was after the personality of the girl and whether she would enjoy and fit in with the life. As one army general observed, 'One had to have an appetite for adventure.' How true that was, the unexpected had to be welcomed. I did relief theatres for emergencies and leave in BAOR and sometimes had less than a day's notice but enjoyed the surprise! By trial and error I found the question to ask to find the answer was: 'If Matron came to you on the ward at 4 pm and said would you like to go off duty and start packing as you were going to Germany/Cyprus/Singapore for some emergency within forty-eight hours, how would you feel about it?' The answers spoke volumes. Some faces would fall and the eyes glaze over and the words Oh No! No! No! would be uttered. Other faces would light up and Great! Super! Fantastic! would issue forth and you could be on to a winner.

Over the next year the WRAC sergeant recruiters would telephone and say that Miss so and so had been commissioned and I would put a tick by the name at the back of the desk diary. In November 1970 the colonel asked me to write a brief for the director of army recruiting as there was to be a special manpower meeting at HQ. I'd never done one before but I assumed numbers would be involved and I had to go back to the names at the back of the diary and start counting the ticks. To my surprise eight had already been commissioned and twenty were in the pipeline. I also stated that in many instances the image of the army sister remains 'an old battle axe of a matron on a parade ground' for those without any contact with us, and the only way to get rid of that image was by personal contact with an enthusiastic officer who had done service overseas and could put across the many advantages of the QAs.

In December '71, just before I left, we had increased our numbers by nearly one hundred sisters over the *whole* country in four years but I think Western Command had helped a great deal as it was a good recruiting ground.

In the first week of August 1970 there was to be a Military Silver Exhibition at the Town Hall in Chester. The public relations staff at Western Command suggested a private viewing by two civilian nurses of the Florence Nightingale communion set held by our museum at the training centre. On one of my visits to the centre with a party of WRAC recruiters and potential QAs I was to transport it safely to Chester. What a responsibility! I was also to bring the set of medals of Dame Maud McCarthy, Matron-in-Chief to the British Expeditionary Force who had remained in France and Flanders throughout the First World War. The retired nursing officer at Saighton Camp, Major Pegg QARANC, was asked to join us for the photographs.

The inscription read: 'This Chalice with two patens and flagon of silver were given by Miss Nightingale for use at soldier services at Scutari Asia AD 1854 to Rev. Canon Sadin late CF and by him left for use in Malta to the senior CE Chaplain AD 1884'.

I attended the Champagne party and preview of the exhibition which was superb but far too crowded to be able to appreciate it fully and I slipped back later in the week to have a more leisurely look. I then had the responsibility of returning the set and medals on my next visit with a party of girls.

In 1970 we had a replacement film called 'Scarlet and Grey' which was also very good and the girls loved it – some finding they were a bit squeamish at the operating scenes but they loved the babies and the children's wards and many clapped when it was over. We had to cope with a huge cross section of different types of school with varied educational standards. One would go from the sublime to the ridiculous in one day's work, which kept one on one's toes. Certain areas were becoming very informal and entering some schools it was getting difficult to recognise the teachers in jeans and T-shirts from the pupils themselves. Some secondary modern schools were immaculate and even had two smartly turned-out girls in uniform to greet you on the steps and take you to the headmistress's office. Most of the schools were reasonably organised but in some one had to take charge, put your own projector up and get going with the talk.

I found the girls very likeable even in the rough areas of Liverpool and I never went to a school where I would not have wanted to go back to. Some thirteen- to fifteen-year-olds had a limited attention span and if you didn't get their attention in the first sixty seconds you might as well pack up and go home. In those circumstances I used to start by saying, 'Girls, you will be pleased to know that army girls are no longer issued with three pairs of khaki bloomers or ETBs - elastic top and bottoms as they are listed on the quartermaster's store list - you are now given £30 to go to Marks & Spencer's and buy three sets of pretty underwear.' That usually got their attention and I moved on quickly. At the end of the talk and film, questions followed such as 'What time do you have to be in at night?' and 'Can we try yer 'at on Miss?' My hat would go up and down the desks to great jollity. When leaving I used to put my hat back on my head wondering if I was taking anything extra home but I never did!

Once going to a school way out in the Staffordshire countryside I was taken to the common room for coffee and more than half the staff were smartly turned-out male teachers. They immediately got to their feet and queued up to shake hands, they had been expecting a male major and had quite a shock when I walked in. An interesting coffee break!

One evening I was invited to a grammar school near Oldham to take part in a parent's evening with girls to give information on local government, insurance, ophthalmic work and women's services. On arrival, the headmistress asked me if I would mind coming on last to which I agreed of course. It was a very hot evening and these lectures were not exactly scintillating with much repetition and speakers not knowing how to finish. I really felt very sorry for the families. Looking round I realised by the age of the fathers they would have either served in the war or done some National Service so I decided to wake them all up with the 'khaki bloomers' opening which was greeted with a roar! At the end the head thanked me and said the army always had good lecturers! I had a long journey home and it was very late but I felt it was worth the effort.

In 1971 I visited a three-year-old secondary modern school in a deprived area at the back of Scotland Road, Liverpool, to speak to forty girls in the fourth year at 9.15 am. That meant being on the road by 7.30 am to avoid John Summers Steel Works change of shifts at Queensferry and get through the Mersey Tunnel in the rush hour.

The girls were tough, likeable and responsive and both films went down well, particularly offering girls work with no GCSE qualification. It was followed by quite a good question time but one child who stood up asked the question: 'Did you have to stay up all night when babies cried?' No one laughed, this was too close to home for some of them. The young girl was the size of a nine year old, undernourished and with dark circles under her eyes reminding me now of the poster for 'Les Miserables'.

I gently explained about our shifts and night duty where the girls sleep in the day so no one has to get up at night when the babies cry. When I got back to the staff room with the teacher I asked her why that child had asked that question. She was the eldest of five, the youngest being eighteen months. Father had gone off to look for work, mother worked in a pub and didn't get home until after 1 am so she was the one who had to get up when the babies cried. That child haunted me and I just hoped she had got enough from my talk and films to have the courage at sixteen years old to go into the recruiting office in Liverpool and ask what was available for her or she would be married at sixteen years and still getting up at night when the babies cried.

One day when my husband was home I had been completing my monthly reports all morning and part of the afternoon but I had an appointment at 3 pm at the convent eight miles away to introduce myself to the mother superior and leave a couple of brochures. I would only be away about three-quarters of an hour so I said, 'Put the kettle on at 3.15 for tea – I'll be back.' I arrived promptly and as I put my hand out to ring the bell the door opened and the mother superior put her hand on my shoulder saying, 'So pleased to see you Major Thomas, the dancing teacher hasn't come and I'd like you to speak to the upper school!' I had no film, only a briefcase with some brochures in. I was shown to the gym where there were about sixty girls from thirteen to sixteen years old. This convent was run by a very down-to-earth headmistress but one who did not believe in giving careers advice to her girls, rather on turning out good citizens able to cope with the world. The girls were a delight but had never had anyone to speak to them about careers. I spoke about WRAC officers and other ranks as well as the QAs. I was besieged with questions on everything including how to become an air hostess, train as a children's nanny, work with horses, animals, you name it and they asked about it. I filled a clipboard paper with the list and promised to ask the local careers officer for all the information and return it to the school!

The school had no sixth form but the headmistress had suggested that a Catholic boys' independent school in Hereford should take her suitably qualified girls for two years. She fought a battle with the reverend fathers and won and it was going to start shortly. I was given tea before I left and can only assume I was invited into this convent because I was a nurse. I arrived home at 4.45 pm being greeted on the doorstep by my husband saying the kettle burned out at 3.30 pm!

On leave at the beginning of August I was struck down by a viral infection doing the rounds, which gave me labyrinthitis (acute dizziness) and which made it impossible to drive the car, and photophobia (aversion to light), which made me want to hide under the blankets. The virus was affecting the public school at Ruthin where we lived (twenty-five miles from Chester and dead centre of my area) and they were concerned that it might be an outbreak of meningitis, photophobia being one of the signs. I slowly improved although didn't feel 100% for some weeks and limited my travelling but I was back to normal work by early September.

Chatting to Gwen, a friend and neighbour, she announced I could be pregnant and should see a doctor! Not being a midwife I had ignored other subtle signs and symptoms putting everything down to the virus. To say her remark was a shock was an understatement and I decided to do as she suggested and her diagnosis was spot on. This was completely unplanned and as I had just passed my sixteen years service on August 10th giving me a minimum army pension I wasn't sure that the MOD would believe me!

These were the days before routine scans and I was quite apprehensive thinking that approaching thirty-nine years of age I could be subject to some congenital problems such as spina bifida or Down's syndrome but of course never mentioned it to anyone least of all my husband, but it was worrying. I continued working normally until nearly

Christmas when I was due for some leave and resigning on family grounds on the 1st January 1972. I was dined out at the castle officers' mess and thanked everyone for their help and support over the last four years. They had been a marvellous team to work with and I had thoroughly enjoyed my job with them. This should have been the end of my 'memories' but little did I know what a momentous year 1972 would turn out to be.

In the early hours of the morning on April 8th I was safely delivered of a beautiful baby boy twenty-two inches long and weighing in at 9lbs. 13oz. Listening to his lusty cries all the way down the corridor to the nursery I knew I had a very fit baby for which I was truly thankful. One of the many cards was from Margaret McDermott with the remark, 'Not bad for a very elderly primapara!' The midwives do tend to think you are over the hill at twenty-five years old! We were blessed with a happy, contented baby who never gave us a sleepless night. As Margaret would frequently say, 'God was kind'. My husband by now had 'swallowed the anchor' and was working locally ashore.

One morning in early June my husband brought in a brown envelope, similar to what the paper bill came in saying, 'There's some funny letters on this.' I looked at it and remarked that someone at MOD had confused me with Lt. Col. Enid M Thomas with whom I had worked in theatre at Millbank. On opening it I found it was from Brigadier Barbara Gorden heading 'My dear Margaret' and congratulating me on being awarded the ARRC (Associate member of the Royal Red Cross) in the Queen's Birthday Honours for my work in recruiting. I promptly burst into tears over the cornflakes and for once I was speechless. Later would come instructions for the investiture at the palace in November.

In July we went to Sheffield to celebrate my mother's eightieth birthday by taking her out to lunch. Baby Ian came too of course and after waking up in his pram laughed and gurgled at us through the window of the hotel restaurant.

On August 4th we were preparing to go to Anglesey to celebrate my mother-in-law's eightieth birthday when my husband Alan came in from the car, said he didn't feel very well, climbed the stairs and had a severe heart attack on the bed. The GP came quickly – he had been treating him for angina but looked very solemn and shook his head, the ambulance came and then had to battle with twenty miles of holiday traffic to the nearest coronary care unit at the Alexandra Hospital at Rhyl. No paramedics in those days to monitor and start treatment.

My lovely neighbours sorted me out, Elwyn looked after Ian who luckily had just been fed and Gwen put me into her car and followed the ambulance. On arrival at the hospital the ambulance men were just coming out of the lift with the trolley and I asked if Mr Thomas was still alive – 'Yes and the doctors are with him' – and for the first time I thought he had a chance. I think it was then that I mentally pulled down the blind over my previous sixteen years, other challenges now lay ahead. I had a four-and-a-half-month-old baby, a very sick husband and I could be a widow at any time.

For the next month I did a round trip of forty miles every afternoon between Ian's feeds to visit 2 pm to 4 pm. The neighbours in the close were wonderful and had Ian in turn almost every day. Sister gave me permission to take Ian with me to the unit and then the ward if no one was available to look after him. His blonde complexion, deep blue eyes and long black eye lashes charmed everyone from doctors, nurses and patients alike and he seemed to be mesmerised by the change of scenery and I never remember him crying at all.

At the end of the month Alan came home for convalescence and rehabilitation, which took three months. He got back to work but had two more attacks and in 1981 had a successful triple bypass when for the first time he could play cricket with Ian. He survived twenty-one years and saw Ian grow up, which is what he had aimed for.

Epilogue

Keeping out of Mischief

In November 1972 Ian went to stay with Clare and Dom in Anglesey and on a beautiful sunny morning with a cloudless sky and a distinctive nip in the air, my husband, my mother and I reported to Buckingham Palace at 10 am just as the impressive high gates were opening. My mother and Alan had a front-row seat as we were early and sat directly in front of Her Majesty while I waited in the anterooms. A young soldier looking a bit lost and by himself caught my attention and I walked over to chat with him, I asked him who he had come with (his mum) and what he was here for. They had been on exercise in the Arctic region and two men from a group of three soldiers had fallen into sub-zero waters with survival expectancy of two minutes. He had rescued the soldiers and survived in the water for eight minutes. It made me feel very humble.

Her Majesty asked me if I was still in the service and I said, no, I had an eight-and-a-half-month-old baby boy at home and she replied that that would keep me out of mischief!

We returned to the junior officers club at Eaton Square

for lunch with Joyce and Hamish, both friends from Colchester days, and later that afternoon Stephen (again a friend from Colchester days) had invited us to tea at his flat in Marsham Street close to Millbank. What a lovely day and beyond my wildest dreams.

That really is the end of my memoirs, recorded for my son who knew little of what his mum did before he arrived. I have been giving *selected* excerpts to women's groups for over twenty years and I now split it up into four talks. The second talk about the individuals I met, the happy, sad, sometimes hilarious happenings can still make me laugh or cry but I always finish with General Montgomery's talk when addressing his officers in North Africa in the War.

'The most important people in the British Army are the nursing sisters and the padres. The sisters because they tell The Men they matter to us and the padres because they tell The Men they matter to God and it is The Men that matter.'

To me it was the greatest privilege to nurse 'The Men'.